Advanced
Cinematherapy

Also by Nancy Peske and Beverly West

Bibliotherapy: The Girl's Guide to Books for Every Phase of Our Lives

Cinematherapy: The Girl's Guide to Movies for Every Mood

Frankly Scarlett, I *Do* Give a Damn!: Classic Romances Retold

And under the pseudonym Lee Ward Shore:

How to Satisfy a Woman Every Time on Five Dollars a Day

Meditations for Men Who Do Nothing (and Would Like to Do Even Less)

Advanced Cinematherapy

The Girl's Guide to Finding Happiness One Movie at a Time

Nancy Peske and Beverly West

A DELL TRADE PAPERBACK

A DELL TRADE PAPERBACK

Published by
Dell Publishing
a division of
Random House, Inc.
1540 Broadway
New York, New York 10036

Dell Books may be purchased for business or promotional use or for special sales. For information please write to: Special Markets Department, Random House, Inc., 1540 Broadway, New York, NY 10036.

DTP and the colophon are trademarks of Random House, Inc.

LIBRARY OF CONGRESS CATALOGING-IN-PUBLICATION DATA
Peske, Nancy K., 1962–
    Advanced cinematherapy : the girl's guide to finding happiness one movie at a time /
Nancy Peske and Beverly West.
        p. cm.
    Includes index.
    ISBN 0-440-50915-7
    1. Motion pictures for women—Catalogs.   2. Video recordings—Catalogs.
I. West, Beverly, 1961–   II. Title
PN1995.9.W6 P47 2002
791.43'75'082—dc21   2001047269

Printed in the United States of America
Published simultaneously in Canada
March 2002

FFG   10 9 8 7 6 5 4 3 2 1

For Sean McKenna, my strongest link,
and the most macho guy I know.
—Bev

For George and Dante,
who make my life more magical than the movies.
—Nancy

Acknowledgments

We would like to thank our editors, Kathleen Jayes and Danielle Perez, for their support and encouragement. We'd also like to welcome the newest member of the Cinematherapy team, our television agent, Myles Hazleton, and a very special thanks to our literary agent, Neeti Madan, for her creativity, confidence, clever strategizing, and excellent taste in trendy gin joints.

Bev: Thanks to Pam and Lily Eisermann, my two favorite unmanageable women; to John Giuliano, for bringing so much fun and period elegance to my life; and to Mark Wisneski, who helps my garden grow. Thanks to Sean McKenna for being right about just about everything just about always, and to that adorable Jason Bergund, who sweeps me off my feet. Thanks also to Mom and Dad, to Richie Fusco, and to Ellen Rees and Joe Kolker, my two favorite Freudians. Finally, a very special thanks to my main woman Nancy, for always standing by my side and being such good company on our excellent adventure.

Nancy: Thanks to my husband, George Darrow, for surrendering the remote and seeking out chick flicks for me at the video store; my son, Dante, for letting me hog the VCR even when he was jonesing for a Teletubbies tape; Mom, Carol Peske, and Phyllis Curott for their love, support, insights, and movie suggestions; Keonaona Peterson for her friendship and her tips on great flicks; Jennifer Flannery and Chris and Carol Mahon for their cheerleading; the ever-stylish Hellie Neumann for inspiring the Hoopskirt Dream sidebar series; and especially, thanks to my cowriter and identical cousin, Bev, who makes me grateful every day that I have her for a friend, relative, and business partner, 'cause I can't imagine having any more fun than we're having!

Contents

Introduction

If you're feeling invisible or unloved and in need of a little understanding or hope for the future, take heart! The inspiration and insight you're looking for is no further away than your own remote control.

We understand that women watch movies differently than guys do. For us, movies are more than just entertainment: they're self-medication that can help cure anything from an identity crisis to the codependent blues.

So whether you're on the verge of yet another major life change, recovering from a rough day at the office, or trying to unlock the mystery of the opposite sex, Cinematherapy can help you laugh at your troubles or confront your issues, and inspire you to grow. Most important, indulging in a movie gives us women two hours to cuddle up in a pair of fuzzy slippers, be in charge of our own remote controls, and nurture ourselves for a change. Really, Cinematherapy is like a bubble bath for the soul.

In our previous book, **Cinematherapy: The Girl's Guide to Movies for Every Mood**, we offered readers a panoply of movies to match their every emotional state. Now we've taken it a step further and written **Advanced Cinematherapy: The Girl's Guide to Finding Happiness One Movie at a Time.** This time around, we categorized movies according to some of the specific issues and dysfunctional dynamics that we all wrestle with in our day-to-day lives. For instance, we review films that address our trust issues, which can make us vacillate between gullible and hyperparanoid. We also look at Codependency Movies, which teach us that unless we hold to our boundaries we will find ourselves trying to balance on one foot in the whittled-down space that has become our turf. We've included movies that lift us up and help us find meaning in the mundane, as well as movies that reveal difficult truths, like the fact that the more we try to control our world, the more likely it is that fate will strand us on a deserted island hundreds of miles from Coast Guard search teams.

You say you're in the midst of a full-blown midlife, flapping-triceps crisis? Watch a Midlife Crisis Movie like *Shirley Valentine*, and be reassured that it ain't over 'til the fat lady goes to Greece and jumps feet first into oceans of sensuality. Feeling in need of a little wind beneath your wings? Watch a Role Model Movie, like *Erin Brockovich*, about heroines who find their place in the sun, and spring into full bloom. Or if you're feeling like a welcome mat on the doorstep of life, watch one of our Diva Movies and learn how to rule your realm with an iron fist without breaking a nail.

Advanced Cinematherapy includes reviews of both classic and modern movies that confront women's issues. We've also included just-for-fun sidebars, like quotes we'd like printed on a coffee mug, famous last words, Stupid Guy Quotes (and Stupid Girl Quotes too, because it takes two to tangle), and Hoopskirt Dreams movies that feature delicious outfits we wish we had in our closets and budgets.

Then again, we felt it was important to warn you against some of those well-hyped alleged "chick flicks" that on closer examination turned out to have some downright dysfunctional psychological messages about how to deal with life's conflicts. Throughout the book, you'll find reviews of these psychologically dubious flicks in our sidebar series Freudian Slipups. And our Reel to Real series points out the often yawning chasm between our real historical heroines and their depiction in the movies.

So whether you're ready to dive in and confront your demons or escape to a more perfect world where men really do change and chocolate never goes to your thighs, in **Advanced Cinematherapy** you'll find films that will match your mood and leave you feeling like you just emerged from the day spa, renewed, replenished, and fully exfoliated.

Nancy Peske and Beverly West
May 2001

You may write to the authors at *BevandNancy@aol.com* or in care of Dell Trade Paperbacks.

Chapter 1

She's All That and a Bag of Fries: Diva Movies

Does it seem that having it all means doing it all, but no matter how much you do, it still isn't enough, and at the end of a very long day, you wind up with a whole lot of nothing for your effort but a cramp in your lower lumbar?

Listen, what are you killing yourself for? Take a tip from the great divas of the silver screen and let somebody else worry about the gory details for a change. We all deserve star billing in our own lives every once in a while, so if you're feeling overwhelmed, settle in for some self-pampering Cinematherapy style, where for a few hours at least, you get to have it all without doing a blessed thing.

So go on. Take off those work gloves, break out the ruby nail polish, and watch one of these Diva Movies featuring unmanageable heroines who put their own needs first, ruling their roosts with an iron fist, without ever breaking a nail.

■ *Gentlemen Prefer Blondes* (1953)
Stars: Marilyn Monroe, Jane Russell
Director: Howard Hawks
Writers: Anita Loos, Joseph Fields, Charles Lederer

Who better than the original Material Girl to teach us all a little something about looking out for number one? This flick stars the eternally iconic Marilyn Monroe as the immortal little girl from Little Rock, Lorelei Lee, who sets her tiara for a rich husband to satisfy her insatiable appetite for diamonds.

Lorelei is undeterred from her bottom-line–driven approach to matrimony by her less mercenary friend Dorothy Shaw (Jane Russell), who manages, in the course of one sea voyage, to fall in love with the entire men's Olympic relay team including the shot-putter. The plot employs the usual Hollywood high jinks to generate hysteria: mistaken identities, men in women's lingerie, large derrieres and small portholes, and chorus girls in Schiaparelli-inspired S&M gear hanging from the chandeliers. You get the picture. But what this movie is really about is the incomparable Marilyn, who infuses her dumb blonde routine with a fourteen-karat authenticity that has never been equaled by her cubic zirconian imitators.

What's most notable about this movie, though, is that the fortune-seeking Lorelei actually marries her fortune. This is a great movie to watch when you're having a few entitlement issues and need to remind yourself that all us little girls from Little Rock, or Boise, or even Manhattan, are entitled to the best, and that the true definition of a diva is a woman who knows how to take care of herself.

■ *Torch Song* (1953)
Stars: Joan Crawford, Michael Wilding
Director: Charles Walters
Writers: John Michael Hayes, Jan Lustig

Joan Crawford plays the alpha diva in this bitch-on-wheels performance that features inspiring fashions, even more inspiring temper tantrums, and Joan in blackface with rhinestones on her eyelids and an Afro wig. This is a getup that only a woman with the self-

Marilyn Melt-Aways

If a girl is spending all her time worried about all the money she doesn't have, how's she going to have any time for being in love?

★ Marilyn Monroe as Lorelei Lee in
Gentlemen Prefer Blondes

Real diamonds! They must be worth their weight in gold!

★ Marilyn Monroe as Sugar Kane in *Some Like It Hot*

I just got to feel that whoever I marry has some real regard for me, aside from all that lovin' stuff.

★ Marilyn Monroe as Cherie in *Bus Stop*

---

possession of Joan Crawford could carry off, and frankly, we're not even sure she gets away with it.

In *Torch Song*, Joan plays dancer/singer Jenny Stewart and no one, but no one, will get in her way as she valiantly strives to please her audience. And if that means that the male dancer who keeps tripping over her outstretched right leg as she strikes a pose gets ground into the floor like a half-smoked cigarette under her elegantly pointed toe, well, that's show-biz. *Somebody fix me a drink and get me a new boy—pronto!*

It takes a poised, talented, patient, and psychologically astute musical arranger to rein Jenny in and teach her to trot like a good girl. Tye Graham (Michael Wilding) is all those things, and he sees through to her vulnerable and lovable inner core, despite his being blind (the war, you know) and thus unable to appreciate her astonishing ability to match all her lounging robes to her mules (really, have you *tried* to find lemon mules lately?). To Tye, Jenny is a gypsy Madonna, a vibrant and fiery performer who simply needs the love of a good man, a man who knows that, as the butler says, "The easy ones are no fun." Ooo, girl, you got that right.

Watch this one when you're feeling in need of just a little understanding and appreciation for your specialness, or if you're looking for some fabulous fashion guidance (check out that navy-into-sunset-splash-orange dress—too *Vogue*).

Diva Diamonds

Jack, get this through your head. The first time I ever sang I fell in love with the audience. I've been in love with the audience ever since. I'm going to give them the best that's in me no matter who, what, or when tries to stop me, including you.
★ Joan Crawford as Jenny Stewart in *Torch Song*

Oh, for goodness' sake. Get down off that crucifix, someone needs the wood.
★ Guy Pearce as Felicia in *The Adventures of Priscilla, Queen of the Desert*

You think that because I'm beautiful I don't have feelings. Well, you're wrong. I'm an actress. I've got all of them!
★ Goldie Hawn as Elise Eliot in *The First Wives Club*

▪ *The First Wives Club* (1996)
Stars: Bette Midler, Goldie Hawn, Diane Keaton
Director: Hugh Wilson
Writer: Robert Harling, based on the novel by Olivia Goldsmith

This movie is like a cinematic trifecta featuring three, three, three divas in one. Estranged college girlfriends Brenda (Bette Midler), Elise (Goldie Hawn), and Annie (Diane Keaton) reunite twenty-five years later, after the suicide of a mutual friend. Over a Manhattan-style ladies' lunch of low-fat vertical New Wave fusion food and way too many

Bloody Marys, they discover they are just like their dear departed friend: they are all wounded soldiers in retreat from the atrocities of a male midlife crisis.

Just as they pledged to a sorority years ago, they pledge to help each other make their ex-husbands pay for their love crimes—in spades. Strengthened by their sisterhood, and drunk on vigilante justice, they gradually rediscover their inner divas and rise, like three fabulous phoenixes, from the ashes of their seventh-inning slump.

The First Wives Club is a scorned woman's all-you-can-eat brunch, featuring a selection of vicarious revenge delicacies that will satisfy even the most exacting and voracious thirst for blood. Sit down to this diva buffet with your best girlfriends and a Bloody Mary or two. And if you happen to break into a spontaneous and well-choreographed girl group number such as "You Don't Own Me," go for it! Just be sure to tip generously.

Freudian Slipups

Dark Victory (1939)
Stars: *Bette Davis, George Brent, Geraldine Fitzgerald, Humphrey Bogart*
Director: *Edmund Goulding*
Writer: *Casey Robinson, based on the play by George Emerson Brewer, Jr., and Bertram Bloch*

How can we not admire Judith Traherne (Bette Davis), a Long Island rich girl who combines a WASP sensibility with a distinctly French, free-spirited joie de vivre? She's full of sparkle and verve, drinking in the champagne of life, ready to leap over the tallest fence with her horse. Ah, if only she didn't have pesky headaches, double vision, an inability to concentrate, memory loss, and severe nerve damage in her right hand that prevents her from feeling a cigarette burning down to the stub. Well, she'll simply set her shoulders back, take to using a

. . . continued

cigarette holder, and be gay, gay, gay. No wonder that upon meeting her, brain surgeon Frederick Steele (George Brent) decides to perform one last operation before he retires to Vermont. Sadly, he is unable to cure the woman he is starting to fall in love with. Yes, one day, it will all go dark, this bright light will quietly dim, and those Max Steiner orchestrations will reach such a stunning crescendo that you'll be scrambling for the volume-lowering button on the remote.

It's hard to imagine a gal who stares down death with as much aplomb as Judith, but we've gotta wonder about a doc who starts cutting into a woman's gray matter without going over the basics with her—like, say, her diagnosis and prognosis. And we worry that when Judith realizes the end is near, she stoically faces death alone and denies her loved ones any sense of closure.

Hey, we're all for bravery in the face of the inevitable, but we think this WASP stiff-upper-lip thing is a bit much. And Steele's little words of wisdom to her friend: "We can never even think about it. In fact, we don't even talk about it . . . we just pretend that nothing's going to happen"? Definitely an attitude that works better on the screen than in the real world.

▪ *Cabaret* (1972)
Stars: Liza Minnelli, Michael York, Joel Grey
Director: Bob Fosse
Writers: Jay Presson Allen, Joe Masteroff, John Van Druten, based on the book Berlin Stories *by Christopher Isherwood*

Cabaret turns the spotlight on one of divadom's primary truths: if you keep your eyes glued to the disco ball, life can seem like a perpetual cocktail party, even if you're on the verge of the Holocaust and you and your boyfriend are cheating on each other with the same rich international playboy.

Sally Bowles (Liza Minnelli) is an American heiress in self-imposed exile in prewar Berlin. There she engages in various acts of harmless adolescent rebellion. She wears green nail polish in a shade called Divine Decadence, slams prairie oysters at 10 A.M., and performs socially provocative numbers at a questionable local watering hole, accompanied by an androgynous and darkly ingratiating master of ceremonies (Joel Grey) who is really just a tap-dancing metaphor for the ultimate decline of Western civilization. Our kind of diva, right?

Abruptly the movie takes a sentimental turn, and seems to suggest that beneath our diva's gravity-defying lashes, blood-red lipstick, and vampire-white foundation is just a little girl from Kansas who needs to learn to be content to stay in her own monochromatic backyard, and not go looking for her heart's desire.

But then we and Sally get real. We realize that this is not a frothy romp that winds up with a reformed diva snuggled up in a cozy bungalow in Cambridge. This is a Brechtian commentary on the dangers of denial and the horror of the Holocaust—and the terrible cost of the disco era. And that's not Dorothy up there in the ruby slippers. That's Liza with a Z, on the verge of her Studio 54 period, and last call is at least ten years away.

This is a great movie to watch when you're on the brink of a personal world war. Pop in *Cabaret*, paint your fingernails green, and dance in the face of disaster along with Liza, without ever having to confront the inevitable morning after.

Diva Diamonds

When a dress costs over a hundred bucks, it's a frock!
   ★ Barbara Stanwyck as Kay Arnold in *Ladies of Leisure*

What should an ex-wife do? Spend her days doing good deeds? Going to bed at night with suitable books?

      ★ Norma Shearer as Jerry in *The Divorcée*

Girls who start with breakfast don't usually end up with supper.
   ★ Claudette Colbert as Franzi in *The Smiling Lieutenant*

Nancy's Momentous Minutiae:
Too Divine

Silent-screen actress Clara Bow, known as the "It Girl," had a penchant for zipping around Hollywood in a convertible, accompanied by her red Chow dogs, whose fur matched her own locks.

On a publicity junket for the flick *Personal Property*, Jean Harlow brought on board the train her mother, her hairdresser, her publicist, twenty-one pieces of luggage that included several gowns from the movie, and five-gallon bottles of spring water to wash her hair with.

When doing love scenes, Errol Flynn would cast his gaze on his leading lady's hairline instead of her face because he was convinced that somehow this made his eyes look bigger and more attractive.

▪ *My Little Chickadee* (1940)
Stars: Mae West, W. C. Fields
Director: Edward F. Cline
Writers: W. C. Fields, Mae West

Mae West, the founding mother of the American diva, stars as Flower Belle Lee, a voluptuous prairie rose with a bad reputation that she completely deserves. Flower Belle is run out of her small town of origin by a sour-faced busybody (Margaret "Wicked Witch of the West" Hamilton) because she is suspected of fooling around with the handsome Masked Bandit who has been terrorizing the countryside. And those suspicions are right on the money.

But Flower Belle sneaks out at night to meet her paramour on a remote hillside on the wrong side of town, only to come face-to-face with the authorities, who insist that she become respectable and get hitched already. Flower Belle meets Cuthbert J. Twillie (W. C. Fields) on a train, and ties the knot with him because he is carrying a bag full of money. Once in the honeymoon suite, however, she discovers that all that glitters is not necessarily Cuthbert.

As is the case with most Mae West vehicles, this is not a movie about plot. It's about watching two groundbreaking comic geniuses going head-to-head in a heavyweight bout of one-liners, and about the inimitable Mae West, who created the mold for opinionated, self-directed, full-figured heroines who take what they want from the world and don't make any apologies.

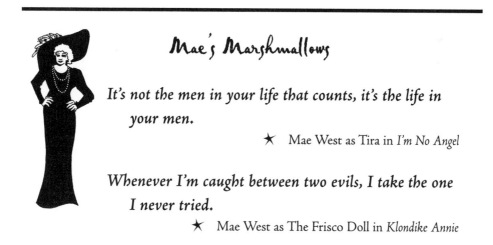

Mae's Marshmallows

It's not the men in your life that counts, it's the life in your men.

★ Mae West as Tira in *I'm No Angel*

Whenever I'm caught between two evils, I take the one I never tried.

★ Mae West as The Frisco Doll in *Klondike Annie*

■ *Mr. Skeffington* (1944)
   Stars: Bette Davis, Claude Rains, Marjorie Riordan
   Director: Vincent Sherman
   Writers: Julius J. Epstein, Philip G. Epstein, based on the novel by
      Elizabeth von Arnim

Alright, so Fanny Skeffington (Bette Davis) is a tiny bit shallow—while world wars rage and the stock market crashes, she's getting yet another facial and fussing over her many hats. Eventually a self-centered, vain, mercenary rich bitch like Fanny has to get her come-uppance, of course, and it's a safe bet that it's going to involve losing her looks one day and hence her drawing room full of clucking male admirers, but at least she gets in a couple of good decades of diva fun before that happens.

Still, for all Fanny's many character flaws she's got one terrific trait that everyone seems to overlook: her forthrightness. Yes, Fanny matter-of-factly and even humorously accepts the truths of life and speaks them aloud—except, of course, for the one that she finds most threatening, which is that her lovely face has begun to sink to the floor. As for Fanny's shallow nature, maybe if she had access to psychotherapists who didn't verbally abuse her, contemptuously suggesting that middle-aged women should give up their notions of romance and crawl back to their estranged husbands, she'd be aging a little more gracefully. Although, to be honest, we kind of prefer Miss D. when she's simply having a smashing time and dressing to kill.

Having a bad hair decade? Shake up some Cosmopolitans, give yourself a facial, and indulge in *Mr. Skeffington*. It's a fun reminder that there are times when getting the latest beauty treatment, engaging in a whirlwind social life, and having a jolly good laugh ought to be a gal's number-one priority.

Bette Bites

*Mr. Skeffington (Claude Rains): A woman is
beautiful when she is loved, and only then.*

*Mrs. Skeffington (Bette Davis): Nonsense. A woman is beautiful
if she has eight hours sleep and goes to the beauty parlor every
day. And bone structure has a lot to do with it too.*

★ from *Mr. Skeffington*

There's only one job that matters . . . me!
★ Bette Davis as Miss Stanley Timberlake in *In This Our Life*

Bev's Culinarytherapy: Food for Every Mood

Bad Girl's Buffet

When you're feeling fabulous, there's nothing like a martini and a tray of canapés to offset your magnificent miss thingness. Besides, divas don't have to watch their weight. So when you're in the mood to don the tiara, try out this bad girl buffet, because everything is better when it sits on a Ritz.

The Bad Girl's Martini

3 ounces vodka
1 ounce white crème de cacao
dash peppermint schnapps

a really big hunk of chocolate
cocoa

Tell your houseboy to pour everything except the chocolate and cocoa into a cocktail shaker with ice and for God's sake tell him not to shake too hard or he'll bruise the vodka. Then have him put the chocolate chunk in a martini glass, douse it with the martini, and shake cocoa all over the glass, stem, serving tray, and you. Indulge.

Bad Girl Bonbons

Tell your houseboy to hurry to the nearest high-end chocolaterie and pick you up a pound or two of assorted truffles. And for God's sake tell him to be quick about it. Then sit down and eat the whole box. And remember, life is like a box of chocolates. You never know what you're going to get. So stick your finger in the chocolate first to make sure it's a kind that you like. And if it's one of those horrible fruit cream nougat things, give it to the houseboy.

■ *Guarding Tess* (1994)
Stars: Shirley MacLaine, Nicolas Cage, Austin Pendleton
Director: Hugh Wilson
Writers: Peter Torokvei, Hugh Wilson

Divas don't always come in gold lamé and sequined slippers; sometimes, like Tess Carlisle (Shirley MacLaine), they wear conservative tweeds and sensible shoes. Tess is a popular former first lady, now widowed, who lives surrounded by a battalion of Secret Service men appointed to protect her in her dotage. What lurks beneath the kindly eyes and demure pillbox hats of this American treasure, however, is an unmanageable and steel-willed woman who rules her roost with an iron cane, and is less reminiscent of Barbara Bush than FDR in his heyday.

No one knows her true nature better than her secret special agent in charge, Doug Chesnic (Nicolas Cage), who longs to wear mirrored sunglasses, speak covertly into his wrist, and be where the action is. Instead, Doug is forced to serve a life term in small-town America because Tess has taken a shine to him. What ensues is a wonderful battle of wills between a persnickety old lady and a stoical gun-toting tough guy, who proves to be no match for Tess's nickel-plated resilience.

This is a great movie to watch when you're feeling as if the parade has passed you by. Tess proves that you can be a diva at any age so long as you're not afraid to take life by the lapels, force it to leave its firearms outside the door, and take you golfing in December.

 Warning Label: *Even though the filmmakers found it necessary to give Tess an inoperable brain tumor to make her sympathetic, we real-life women are perfectly entitled to be curmudgeons without contracting a terminal disease, or being kidnapped and buried alive.*

Words to Live By

Life's a bitch so I became one, honey.
★ Philip Seymour Hoffman as Rusty in *Flawless*

■ *Bombshell* (1933)
Stars: *Jean Harlow, Lee Tracy, Frank Morgan, Una Merkel, Ted Healy*
Director: *Victor Fleming*
Writers: *John Lee Mahin, Jules Furthman, based on the play by Mack Crane and Caroline Francke*

People just don't understand, do they? Oh, sure, they see the jewels, furs, and beaded satin gowns, the endorsement deals, the location shoots, the romantic scenes you play with Hollywood's leading men, the mansion in Beverly Hills, the late nights dancing at the Coconut Grove, the hordes of autograph seekers. They think it must be wonderful to be Lola Burns, movie star. But they don't know what a burden it all is. Lola just wants to marry the marquis and lead a quiet life with three sheepdogs in the living room and a baby in the nursery. That's not asking too much, is it? And if she could have all that, Lola could give up motion pictures tomorrow, honest, she could.

Uh-huh.

In this thinly disguised parody of the real Jean Harlow's life, Harlow plays a put-upon starlet who is tired of supporting her father (Frank Morgan), who is often found pickled at 6 A.M.; her brother (Ted Healy), who's been "taking a sleigh ride on the roulette wheel in Tijuana"; and an embezzling secretary (Una Merkel). She's also had it up to her platinum blond wig with the studio publicist (Lee Tracy) whose sole purpose in life is to cook up phony scandals about Lola to place in the papers. Can't these people find another gravy train to latch on to?

Somewhere amid all the histrionics there's a nonsensical plot, but you'll be too distracted watching Lola flip back and forth between hissy fits and starry-eyed dreaming to care. Watch *Bombshell* when you're feeling ignored—you can vicariously enjoy being a flighty drama queen without having to pay the liquor and furrier bills.

Doomed but Inspired Divas

The Rose (1979)
Stars: Bette Midler, Alan Bates, Frederic Forrest
Director: Mark Rydell
Writers: Bo Goldman, Bill Kerby, Michael Cimino

When it comes to a no-nonsense diva with an acid tongue and a heart of gold, very few can rival "The Divine Miss M." Bette Midler made her starring debut in this movie about The Rose, a fictional, Janis Joplin–inspired songstress who overdoses on her own moxie.

Despite Bette Midler's inner diva, which shines through no matter what role we find her in, and despite this character's epic appetite for life, the blues, cowboys, and vodka straight out of the bottle, The Rose's overwhelming and tragically codependent need for love and acceptance ultimately outcroons the diva in her.

This is a good movie to watch when you need to remind yourself that even the most fabulous rock-and-roll goddesses have to learn to draw boundaries or risk giving up their diva crown, because while the sex, drugs, and rock-and-roll may not get you, the unresolved self-esteem issues definitely will.

The-Other-Bette Bytes

Someone is spreading the rumor that being rich is a drag, but let me tell you something honestly: whoever is spreading that rumor is dead-ass broke.

★ Bette Midler as Rose in *The Rose*

Oh I hate this mushy love stuff, man. Wake me up when the killing starts.

★ Bette Midler as Rose in *The Rose*

■ *Hello, Dolly!* (1969)

Stars: Barbra Streisand, Walter Matthau
Director: Gene Kelly
Writers: Ernest Lehman, Michael Stewart

World-class diva Barbra Streisand plays Dolly Levi, a fast-talking, double-dealing, matchmaking diva of the gilded age who proves that love is just as satisfying the second time around, particularly if there are large bank accounts involved.

After her beloved husband dies, Dolly dedicates herself to making everybody else's dreams come true. And what Dolly wants, Dolly gets. In the course of one movie she manages to pair off most of Yonkers and a good portion of the Lower East Side of Manhattan.

But Dolly herself, whose inner light could outshine Broadway, has had her dimmer switch turned down low since her husband's death. Surrounded by all the love and good feeling that she's created, she cranks up the wattage, declares an end to her period of mourning, and takes her sensuality out of dry storage.

Armed with sequins, feathers, a gift for horse-powered gab, and the most fiendishly strategic mind since J. Edgar Hoover, Dolly sets her cap for a misanthrope with a heart of gold, the fabulously wealthy bachelor Horace Vandergelder (Walter Matthau). *Hello, Dolly!* is a great reminder that as long as there is life there is love, and as long as there's love, all of your dreams really can come true, as long as you're willing to march in the parade wearing a couple of really big feathers on your head.

 Warning Label: *We don't hold out great hope for the halogenesque Dolly's future happiness as a woman married to a curmudgeon who will no doubt pinch pennies. We wish Dolly would have kept marching to her own drummer in a parade toward self-fulfillment and independence.*

Barbra Bonbons

Money, pardon the expression, is like manure. It's not worth a thing unless it's spread around, encouraging young things to grow.

★ Barbra Streisand as Dolly Levi in *Hello, Dolly!*

You think beautiful girls are going to be in style forever! I should say not! Any day now they're going to be over! Finished! Then it'll be my turn! ★ Barbra Streisand as Fanny Brice in *Funny Girl*

▪ *Cleopatra* (1963)
Stars: *Elizabeth Taylor, Richard Burton, Rex Harrison*
Directors: *Joseph Mankiewicz and Darryl F. Zanuck*
Writers: *Sidney Buchman, Ranald MacDougall, Joseph Mankiewicz, based on the book by C. M. Franzero*

Nobody defined the word *diva* quite like the original Queen of De Nile, Cleopatra, who not only exhausted the resources of ancient Rome but nearly bankrupted an entire motion picture studio with this exhausting four-hour flick that was the *Waterworld* of its day.

On the surface, this movie chronicles the dramatic reign of Cleopatra (Elizabeth Taylor), who uses her legendary beauty (and impeccable PR instincts) to seduce not one but two Roman emperors—Julius Caesar (Rex Harrison) and Marc Antony (Richard Burton)—and secure her place on the throne of Egypt. But because nobody can walk like an Egyptian quite like Liz Taylor, this homage to excess is less a history lesson than it is a crash course in how to be a diva.

Everything Cleopatra does is designed to make two continents aware of just how fabulous she really is. According to Hollywood's interpretation of the story, Cleopatra's idea of mass transit was riding around in a litter atop a four-story-tall sphinx borne on the backs of an army of buffed male extras, and her concept of fashion was never to wear an outfit twice in the same dynasty. Every time she turns around, Cleopatra is decked out in another sumptuous ensemble, accessorized with crowns and miters, and the most amazing array of eyeshadow ever assembled on one lid. Even the furniture matches her frock. No wonder Cleopatra was the last queen of Egypt. Who could follow an act like this?

When you're feeling like your personal power is being threatened, *Cleopatra* will show you that no matter how mighty the imperial forces that threaten one's reign, there is nothing that can't be conquered by a little imagination and an enormous wardrobe budget.

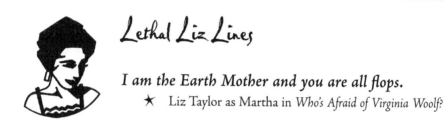

Lethal Liz Lines

I am the Earth Mother and you are all flops.
★ Liz Taylor as Martha in *Who's Afraid of Virginia Woolf?*

You look like a piece of birthday cake, dear! Too bad everyone's had a piece! ★ Liz Taylor as Marina Rudd in *The Mirror Crack'd*

Reel to Real

Despite her glamorous screen image, Cleopatra was actually far from beautiful. In fact, according to her portrait on ancient gold coins, she looked a lot like Ernest Borgnine with a bad nose job. However, the real Cleopatra was very seductive, charismatic, extremely intelligent (she spoke nine languages), and was a notoriously shrewd politician. And her epic theme parties were legendary in the ancient world.

Chapter 2

Let Go, Let God, or Let Him for a Change!: Codependency Movies

When it comes to the people we love, it can be difficult to figure out where we end and the other person begins. He itches, we scratch. She stubs her toe, we say ouch. He loses his job, and we find a second career.

If you're in a committed relationship, it's just about impossible to avoid those moments when your soul mate starts feeling more like a cell mate in the maximum-security prison of dysfunctional love. Even the best of friends and partners can engage us in unhealthy behavior patterns to the point that we find ourselves longing for a stretch in solitary confinement.

When you've got a bad case of the codependent blues, these films, which present the extremes in unhealthy relationships, will give you an objective look at the fusion physics of dysfunction. Why not escape from your self-imposed prison of love by watching someone who is in worse shape than you are?

■ *The Talented Mr. Ripley* (1999)
Stars: Matt Damon, Jude Law, Gwyneth Paltrow
Director: Anthony Minghella
Writer: Anthony Minghella, based on the novel by Patricia Highsmith

This movie puts a haunting spin on the old doppelgänger bait-and-switch routine and reminds us of what can happen when you go looking for your own pot of gold at the end of somebody else's rainbow.

Jude Law plays Dickie Greenleaf, an American prince with a two-thousand-dollar suit and a three-million-dollar smile, who gads about the world charming the pants off people with his puckish emotional unreliability and his father's platinum card. Dickie is that heady mix of irresistible and unattainable that'll set any closet codependent's heart to pounding.

But after all, what normal, red-blooded masochist can resist a blond demigod? Especially one who dwells in a rarefied and palatial villa on a canal by day, and by night, after a few grappas in a smoky club along some insufficiently illuminated Italian byway, makes for a very convincing lead singer in a jazz fusion band. Certainly not the chameleonlike, golden-haired lavatory attendant Tom Ripley (Matt Damon). Tom Ripley, whose special skills include forgery, impersonations, and a remarkable ability to fill out a Princeton blazer just so, is engaged in a perpetual struggle for a higher standard of living, a more sophisticated taste in music, and a psychosexual identity that he can't put on and take off like Dickie's rakish porkpie hat.

The Talented Mr. Ripley is a powerful representation of the trouble we all run into when we focus on somebody else's intimacy issues instead of confronting our own urges to symbolically beat our love objects with a boat oar when they don't live up to our expectations. Watch this one when you need a stern reminder that for better or worse, the reflection that you see in your partner's eyes is usually your own.

■ *Topsy-Turvy* (1999)
Stars: Allan Corduner, Jim Broadbent, Sukie Smith
Director and Writer: Mike Leigh

Codependency issues aren't limited to bungalows in the burbs. Dysfunction insinuates itself into the boardroom, the classroom, or even, in the case of *Topsy-Turvy*, into the creative interplay between two of history's most celebrated and conflicted collaborators, Gilbert (Jim Broadbent) and Sullivan (Allan Corduner).

After the colossal failure of their latest play, *Princess Ida*, Gilbert and Sullivan's creative marriage is strained to the breaking point when Sullivan refuses to collaborate on a new play. Arthur Sullivan, the team's composer, is bored to death with William Gilbert's predictable lyrics, and refuses to put any more effort into the monotonous meanderings of his partner's tired dramatic constructions.

Try though he may, Gilbert cannot seem to come up with anything that will satisfy the inaccessible and perpetually disapproving Sullivan. Desperate to save the partnership, Gilbert rewrites and rearranges himself, performing the musical equivalent of dressing up in Saran Wrap to reignite the passion in his tired romance. But despite Gilbert's best efforts, Sullivan still comes home tired, eats dinner, and falls asleep in front of the television. And so Gilbert learns that that which is not busy being born is busy dying.

Topsy-Turvy is a great movie to watch when you've reached an impasse in your own romantic life, and need to revitalize your own partnership.

Famous Last Words

I'm sorry. I promise I'll never do anything again that you don't want me to do.

★ David Niven as bad boy Tony Halstead
in *Eternally Yours*

▪ *Of Human Bondage* (1964)
Stars: Kim Novak, Laurence Harvey
Director: Ken Hughes, Bryan Forbes
Writer: Bryan Forbes, based on the novel by W. Somerset Maugham

In this wrenching portrait of the toxic force of codependency, Kim Novak plays femme fatale Mildred Rogers, a coarse and haughty working-class girl who aspires to be a lady—

or at least dress like one. Yes, this gal has goals, which we applaud, but then again she has no class, no manners, and no shred of human decency—not that that stops Philip Carey (Laurence Harvey) from falling madly in love with her. Unfortunately, Philip has a major complex because of his clubfoot, and his lack of entitlement sets him up for a love affair that degenerates into a situation worthy of a Jerry Springer showdown.

Of course, when you're an early-twentieth-century British gentleman with a budding medical career, chair throwing isn't an option, so poor Philip just has to grit his teeth while Mildred abuses him. Yet no matter how cruel she becomes, Philip keeps pulling her out of the gutter. Finally she humiliates him so much that he's forced to throw her back into the street where she belongs. And then he comes swooping in on his white horse to rescue her again. And again. And again.

If you want a wince-worthy reminder to spend a little less time thinking about you-know-who and a little more time working on your own entitlement issues, *Of Human Bondage* will bring it all right to the surface.

∞ *So Nice They Did It Twice:* In the original, Bette Davis is wonderfully mean and Leslie Howard will have you wanting to give him a big hug, but it doesn't quite measure up to the 1964 version. Yeah, okay, the antiquated direction is kind of interesting, and we can get past the wretched sound quality, but the overacting and sketchy characterization definitely drag it down.

 Codependent Coffee Mug Sayings

It's okay. I wouldn't remember me either.
★ Kevin Spacey as Lester Burnham in *American Beauty*

■ *The Day of the Locust* (1975)

Stars: Karen Black, Donald Sutherland, Burgess Meredith, William Atherton
Director: John Schlesinger
Writer: Waldo Salt, based on the novel by Nathanael West

Most of us think of codependence in terms of a long-term romance with a significant other. *The Day of the Locust*, Nathanael West's disturbing story about a young artist looking for love and creative fulfillment amid the human rubble of Tinseltown circa 1930, demonstrates that it's possible to have a dysfunctional relationship with an entire city.

Tod Hackett (William Atherton), a young set designer, moves into a hacienda-style apartment complex that suggests a noir version of *Melrose Place*. Despite the fact that Tod is a recent Yale graduate, he still manages to miss the thematic resonance of moving into a unit called "the earthquake cottage" and completely overlooks the horrific conclusion foreshadowed by the cloister of creepy Hollywood down-and-outers that populate his new domain. There's a drunken dwarf, an abusive stage mom, and Adore (Jackie Earle Haley), a hateful, bleached-blonde demon seed, who is perhaps the most grotesque child ever rendered on the silver screen.

The rose amid this tangle of weeds is Faye Greener (Karen Black), the daughter of a vaudevillian snake oil salesman (Burgess Meredith). Faye, an itinerant Hollywood extra, dreams of becoming a movie star someday but winds up instead a helpless victim of her own delusions of glamour. And Tod, being your average red-blooded, highly educated but still obtuse American male, is dazzled by Faye and Hollywood's shiny chrome bumpers without giving a second thought to the inefficient engine beneath the hood.

The Day of the Locust delivers a harsh and evocative lesson in the dangers of unreal expectations and bad faith, which can reduce us all to Tin Pan Alley extras in the sweeping saga of our own life.

Stupid Guy Quotes

Sometimes I wish I could boldly go where no man has gone before . . . but I'll probably stay in Aurora.
★ Dana Carvey as Garth Algar in *Wayne's World*

■ *Casino* (1995)
Stars: Robert De Niro, Sharon Stone, Joe Pesci,
*   James Woods*
Director: Martin Scorsese
Writers: Nicholas Pileggi, Martin Scorsese

While on the surface it seems like *Casino* is a movie about greed, deception, money, power, and murder in gangland Las Vegas, when you look closer, it's actually a movie about greed, deception, money, power, and murder in a world-class codependent marriage.

Ace Rothstein (Robert De Niro), a numbers whiz, is sent by the mob to run a Vegas casino in the seventies. Unfortunately Ace is much better at picking odds and color-coordinated separates than he is at picking wives. Ace marries Ginger (Sharon Stone), a beautiful blond gold digger, who, much like Ace, has a hardball negotiating style, an insatiable appetite for living beyond her means, and really poor instincts when it comes to the opposite sex. They also share severe loyalty and trust issues, intimacy conflicts, an inability to constructively express anger, and startlingly bad taste in interior design. Basically this marriage runs the gamut of destructive syndromes before exploding in a hail of emotional gunfire.

Watch this movie when you need to feel a little bit better about your own *famiglia*. Next to Ace and Ginger, anybody can seem like Ozzie and Harriet.

Those Bad, Bad Boys

If you're feeling tempted to indulge in a codependent and highly toxic love affair with a bad boy, watch one of these movies and savor the feast of dysfunction without having to pay the emotional tab.

■ *Star 80* (1983)
Stars: Mariel Hemingway, Eric Roberts, Cliff Robertson
Director: Bob Fosse
Writer: Bob Fosse, based on the book Death of a Playmate *by Teresa Carpenter*

Sometimes in the search for the fruit of eternal love, we wind up with the one bad apple that spoils the whole bunch girl. Such is the case for Dorothy Stratten (Mariel Hemingway) in this biopic of the 1980 Playmate of the Year who makes the fatal mistake of marrying her first love because she feels sorry for him.

Paul Snider, brilliantly portrayed by Eric Roberts (who, thanks to sister Julia, must know a thing or two himself about the frustration of getting second billing to a close family member), is probably one of the biggest losers in cinematic history. He is like a human pimple, working his way under the skin and erupting at the most inopportune moments, marring even the most flawless of complexions and embarrassing victim and onlookers alike. Paul even manages to make Hugh Hefner (Cliff Robertson) look like landed gentry by comparison. Unfortunately, despite the deep cleansing treatment of a new life, a more respectable lover, and burgeoning career opportunities, Dorothy is unable to rid herself of Paul's chronic emotional acne.

This is a good movie to watch when you're feeling the need to emotionally exfoliate. The salt scrub of Dorothy Stratten's codependence will unclog even the most stubborn of pores and remind us all that good health and proper emotional hygiene are the cornerstones of lasting beauty.

Bette Bites

By the way, our date is off, isn't it? When I didn't hear from you for three years, I leaped to that conclusion. You heel.

★ Bette Davis as Linda Gilman in *June Bride*

■ *Rasputin* (1996)
Stars: Alan Rickman, Greta Scacchi, Ian McKellen
Director: Ulrich Edel
Writer: Peter Pruce

So Rasputin (Alan Rickman) slurps his soup and spills it over his scraggly beard, tells vulgar stories over dinner, exposes himself in public, and regularly gets as drunk as a boiled owl. Yes, his behavior can be infuriating and humiliating, and the price of befriending him may be all that she holds dear. But he can see past the czarina's (Greta Scacchi) hypocrisy and fear, down deep to her very soul. And just when she's ready to dump him once and for all he comes out with a line like "I didn't choose to be holy . . . it frightens me too!" and she wants only to muss his hair and tuck him into eiderdown quilts.

We're not quite sure what the real Rasputin's particular charms were, but we think Alan Rickman, with those sleepy eyes and that drowsy drawl of his, is totally hot in this outrageously cheese-ball flick about the mystical Russian peasant turned prophet. Rasputin's tortured act works wonders on the czarina and for us gals in the home audience as well—think James Dean, only in a vodka-soaked ruffled shirt. Who else but Rickman could bellow lines like "I see more blood . . . I have his pain . . . you will need me!" or "Get on your knees and beg, beg like a peasant with your knees in the dirt, like a beggar or a snake or a thief!" and come off hot, sexy, and dangerous?

So kick back with a little Stoli on the rocks and enjoy a delightfully sleazy seduction by a historical bad boy without having to face a rifle squad of your angry countrymen the next morning.

Reel to Real

In real life, to get rid of this bad boy, Rasputin's enemies had to feed him enough potassium cyanide to kill six men, shoot him in the chest, attack him with an ax, beat him bloody, tie him up, and throw him in the frozen Neva River. Think about it.

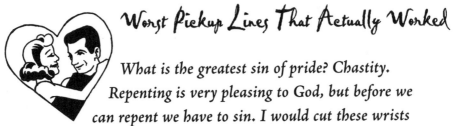

Worst Pickup Lines That Actually Worked

*What is the greatest sin of pride? Chastity.
Repenting is very pleasing to God, but before we
can repent we have to sin. I would cut these wrists
if it would give you a single moment of happiness! Think of
God, my angel. He gave us this pleasure. I talk to God. Kiss
me and you kiss him. Lie with me and you lie with him.*

★ Alan Rickman in *Rasputin*

■ *Love Me or Leave Me* (1955)
   Stars: Doris Day, James Cagney
   Director: Charles Vidor
   Writer: Daniel Fuchs

When you're stuck in the equivalent of a dime-a-dance gin joint and you're tired of being leered at, pawed, and treated like a cheap trinket, it's tempting to jump at the first knight to come to your rescue. But when that knight is a scrawny little street punk extortionist who refers to women as "broads and dames" and demands sexual favors, maybe a blind mailing and a call to a headhunter would provide a better path toward career advancement.

In this biopic of singer Ruth Etting, Doris Day plays Ruth, a gal who dreams of making it big as a singer, but is performing in an era (the 1920s) when a girl needs a guy to make her seem legit—and in a place (Chicago) where street smarts and fists come in handy. Enter a pugilistic punk with good connections—Martin "Marty the Gimp" Snyder (James Cagney)—who offers to make a few calls, and poof, she enters into a Faustian bargain.

For years afterward, as Ruth's star rises, Marty follows her around like a bad credit rating. He constantly reminds her of all she owes him and does his best to keep her self-confidence as low as possible. Etting's loyalty is admirable, but as you watch her wince at each new ugly public scene Marty creates, you'll find yourself wanting to take her out for a couple of martinis and a long conversation about entitlement. Watch this and remember the high cost of getting entangled with a control freak.

■ *Bonnie and Clyde* (1967)
    Stars: Warren Beatty, Faye Dunaway
    Director: Arthur Penn
    Writers: Robert Benton, David Newman III

You know the story. We all do. There you are, just an unassuming, small-town gal with a great set of gams. And then you see him, in a pair of pegged trousers and a wide-brimmed fedora, stealing the family Packard. And before you know it, he's lured you from the protective embrace of your family with promises of adventure, excitement, and romance. Next thing you know you're dressing up in retro-fashions that never seem to wrinkle—and driving around in mint-condition classic sedans with the top down. But eventually it stops being quite as fun as it used to be. And when your eyes are finally opened, you're staring down the double barrel of the law, which has come to put a stop to your emotional larceny.

Bonnie and Clyde is an opera of codependence, and while most of us don't let the bad boys in our lives lead us on a cross-country crime spree, we can probably all relate to Bonnie's preoccupation with dangerous guys with quick triggers who promise us the moon and deliver Swiss cheese.

Watch this movie when you want the thrill of an emotional crime spree, without having to serve a life sentence.

Bette Bites

You're being charming, reasonable, and very boyish. Unless you've changed, that means you're about to drink someone's blood. Probably mine.
    ★ Bette Davis as Linda Gilman in *June Bride*

■ *Magnificent Obsession* (1954)

Stars: Rock Hudson, Jane Wyman, Paul Cavanagh
Director: Douglas Sirk
Writer: Robert Blees

Playboy Bob Merrick (Rock Hudson) is incorrigible, driving his speedboat faster, faster, faster, until boom—his puerile behavior results in the death of a beloved local doctor who by all accounts was a candidate for canonization. At the encouragement of the doc's best pal, Giraud (Paul Cavanagh), the recalcitrant Mr. Merrick is determined to make amends to the widow, Helen (Jane Wyman). But the proud Helen Phillips refuses to take his checks or listen to his apologies, and next thing you know, Bob has inadvertently caused her to go blind (violin crescendo!).

Not willing to leave well enough alone, Bob decides to take his Good Samaritan act to the next level, befriending poor Helen, reading her the funnies (bring on the adorable kid actor for increased awwww-factor in the scene), and even returning to med school just in case someday she might be in need of a lifesaving operation that only he can provide. What a guy!

Want to pretend for a couple of hours that he'd be willing to adopt an entirely different life philosophy all for your sake? Pop in *Magnificent Obsession* and enjoy watching a bad boy try to turn saint without losing his hunky appeal (check out that buffed upper bod and the fabulous do on Rock's head—zoom zoom zoom!).

The Handy Hunk Chart Key

Hunk Ratings:

All-American Bad Boys

WPBM = *Well-Placed Beauty Mark* **RUM** = *Raw Unpredictable Masculinity* **SPA** = *Six-Pack Abs* **RGH** = *Really Good Hair* **DD** = *Drowsy Drawl* **TIWL** = *That Irresistible Wounded Look* **APFM** = *A Poetic Flair for Metaphor* **DMCA** = *Devil-May-Care Attitude* **ASD** = *Aristocratic, Suave, and Debonair* **BE** = *Bedroom Eyes* **EGL** = *Exotic Good Looks* **EMT** = *Eyes Moist with Tears* **FSG** = *Feckless Schoolboy Grin* **PBE** = *Piercing Blue Eyes* **SIN** = *Smoldering, Inscrutable, and Noble* **TSHT** = *That Sexy Homicidal Thing* **CSD** = *Confidently Self-Deprecating*

The Handy Hunk Chart

Edward Norton

SPA, TIWL, DD, SIN, RUM, TSHT

Top Drool Pics: *Primal Fear, American History X, Fight Club*

It's not everybody who can make a multiple murderer with a split personality disorder, a tattooed white supremacist leader, and a proponent of human cockfights with an alter ego who looks like Brad Pitt in a Victoria's Secret bathrobe seem lovable. But then, Edward Norton is no ordinary hunk. For one thing, he seems like he's got a brain in his head. And we understand that in real life he speaks fluent Japanese, which is, like, totally impressive. Put that together with those shy, smoldering eyes, that cockeyed schoolboy grin, and the precision body sculpting that has obviously gone on in the years between *Primal Fear* and *American History X*, and you've got one hot antihero who can straddle good and evil, brains and brawn, and, we imagine, a few other things besides. ■

Josh Hartnett

WPBM, RGH, BE, DMCA, EMT, FSG

Top Drool Picks: *The Virgin Suicides, Here on Earth, Pearl Harbor*

Alright, we realize he's in the male waif stage of his development, and okay, so he's barely legal, but ever since we saw Josh Hartnett do the male version of the Pretty Woman strut down that high school hallway in *The Virgin Suicides* we've been scouring the racks of the video store. Oh, for just one more glimpse of that breathtaking *Tiger Beat* face that managed to communicate its fresh and flawless magnificence despite the most

. . . continued

atrocious pair of aviator sunglasses we've ever seen. Hey, it's not everybody who can make a stroll down a high school hallway emblematic of the doomed but exquisite beauty of youth. Which leads us to believe that Josh is going to be riding up over the hill—with his hair blowing in the first breezes of the summer of the red grass while an overwrought Max Steineresque score swells behind him—in no time. Brad Pitt, move over. ▪

▪ *Eternally Yours* (1939)
Stars: David Niven, Loretta Young, Broderick Crawford
Director: Tay Garnett
Writers: C. Graham Baker, Gene Towne

If there's any man who can get a gal to call off a wedding engagement to some Eggbert at the last minute, it's a magician named The Great Arturo (David Niven) who looks stunning in a tux, performs death-defying stunts, and can hypnotize a rabbit with the mere touch of his long, graceful fingers. No wonder Anita Halstead (Loretta Young) dumps her dull beau Don Barnes (Broderick Crawford), runs off to be Tony's assistant, and follows him all over Europe, even though she's continually finding lipstick on his collar. Istanbul and Melbourne are calling, but Anita is at heart a homebody who just wants a nice farmhouse in Connecticut where the bunnies don't pop out of hats but frolic on the lawn, and hubby's compulsion to defy the laws of nature drives him to keep the weeds from taking over the landscaping around the carport.

If you've been waiting for him to call and tell you he's mended his ways and won't be doing extreme rock climbing anymore, pop this one in and enjoy the fantasy of reforming a lovably naughty boy.

■ *Badlands* (1973)
Stars: Sissy Spacek, Martin Sheen
Director and Writer: Terrence Malick

Badlands is a classic addition to the cross-country serial spree as a metaphor for a bad romance genre.

Kit Carruthers (Martin Sheen) is a young garbage collector with a thirst for celebrity whose only virtue is that he bears an uncanny resemblance to James Dean. He hooks up with Holly (Sissy Spacek), the baton-twirling, diary-keeping teenage daughter of a sign painter, who nevertheless just can't seem to read the writing on the wall.

Holly falls head over heels in love with Kit, a lovable antihero, despite the fact that he shoots her father in cold blood. She also overlooks the fact that Kit torches her family home, and is frequently the victim of psychotic command voices prompting him to slaughter random strangers as a media positioning strategy. Fused together by their outcast status, their emotional illiteracy, their allegorical resonance, and a mutual capacity for epic denial, Kit and Holly wander through the parched and unforgiving Montana Badlands, which, despite the name, they misinterpret as a paradise made for two.

Narrated by the teen magazine ramblings of Holly's junk culture naïveté, their journey lasts as long as their ability to misread just about every signpost on the road to disaster until at last the long arm of the law comes and blasts them from their false euphoria.

This movie, based on the actual story of Charles Starkweather and Caril-Ann

Fugate, is a stunningly crafted portrayal of the dangerous allure of absolute denial. It's a great movie to watch when you're having difficulty navigating your own way out of the badlands, and a good reminder that if you find yourself unable to make out the exit signs on the highway of your own destiny, it's probably a good idea to stop and ask for directions.

 ## Yeah, We Wish

But I did change—the moment you left me I knew I'd never be able to live with anybody else.
★ David Niven as Tony Halstead
in *Eternally Yours*

Chapter 3

I'm Not Waving, I'm Drowning: Rescue Fantasy Movies

Are you caught in the undertow of life and sinking fast, while all your friends are on the shore, too busy playing beach blanket bingo to toss you a life preserver?

If you're tired of breast-stroking your way through the riptide of life, perhaps it's time to relax, lay back on the water, and float for a couple of hours while watching one of these Rescue Fantasy Movies about damsels in distress who are saved in the nick of time by a lifeguard in shining swim trunks—or by that wonderful deus ex machina that comes courtesy of a Hollywood screenwriter. These escapist movies will help you cling to the illusion that if you just tread water long enough, someday your lifeguard will come, and if he doesn't, at least after all that dog paddling you'll have cultivated sufficient upper-body development to swim to shore.

▪ *Houseboat* (1958)
Stars: Sophia Loren, Cary Grant
Director: Melville Shavelson
Writers: Jack Rose, Melville Shavelson

Papa is so unfair, thinks poor Cinzia (Sophia Loren). He keeps her on a short leash when she merely wants to taste the sweet life, to sing and to dance and to laugh from deep within her soul—which is located somewhere below that formidable foundation undergarment that forces all her feminine curves into submission and severely constricts her diaphragm.

In *Houseboat,* Sophia Loren plays a woman desperate to see the world, which in 1958 meant a night on the town and a summer adventure baby-sitting on a houseboat before settling down to suburban domesticity (the feminine force of chaos being a little too scary for your typical moviegoer of the era). She wins the heart of a rather rigid Tom Winters (Cary Grant), a proper sort of papa who doesn't want his three kids "parceled out like cabbages" now that their mother is gone, but who needs to learn a lesson in letting go of the need to control. Only then can the rickety foundations of his life stabilize.

Looking for an easy answer to your yearning for love, adventure, and a sense of meaning? When life's a little too gritty, check out this little Cary Grant romance and pretend that true love conquers all, including the need to expand one's own horizons and one's girdle stays.

> ⚠ Warning Label: *If you're going to be the essence of joie de vivre, the feminine force of creative chaos personified, ready to sweep into the life of the nearest widower and open his heart to possibility and freedom, we suggest that you ditch the girdle!*

Down Boy, Down

She is queen and I know queens. And, oh, has she got herself a nose, and I know noses too. That little schnozzle of hers is the berries, I tell you. And is it cute when she throws that little schnozzle to the high heavens?

★ Robert Williams as Stew Smith in *Platinum Blonde*

■ *The Mask of Zorro* (1998)
Stars: Antonio Banderas, Anthony Hopkins, Catherine Zeta-Jones
Director: Martin Campbell
Writers: John Eskow, Ted Elliott, Terry Rossio, based on a story by Ted Elliott,
Terry Rossio, and Randall Jahnson and a character created by Johnston McCulley

The hardworking people of pre–Gold Rush California are exploited by one governing group after another, but they have faith in a legendary fighter of evil who always shows up in the nick of time. Unfortunately, behind his leather mask, snakelike whip, thrusting sword, and flawless gymnastic moves, our romantic hero (Anthony Hopkins) is just a man like any other. Once the cruel Don Rafael Montero (Stuart Wilson) discovers Zorro's vulnerability, he breaks his enemy's spirit by stealing his infant daughter, Elena, to raise as his own. The people mourn, for now that Zorro is gone, who will save them from the ravages of the greedy dons? And will Elena (Catherine Zeta-Jones), whose only clue about the truth is a vague memory of the scent of the romania flower, be rescued from her childlike illusions about her father and the Spanish government and have the chance to blossom into a self-actualized and confident woman?

Enter a new young hero in a fine leather mask (Antonio Banderas), who like a spirited black stallion needs to enter the lair of the master and learn discipline, control, and the art of proper thrusting. Only then can he avenge his fellow citizens and win the heart of a fiery young woman who can hold her own with a sword and prefers a little sparring before being stripped of her illusions and her mantilla.

In the mood for indulging in romantic notions about being rescued from darkness, oppression, and a near-virginal existence? Slip into *The Mask of Zorro*.

▪ *The Poseidon Adventure* (1972)

Stars: Gene Hackman, Ernest Borgnine, Carol Lynley,
Shelley Winters, Red Buttons, Roddy McDowall
Director: Ronald Neame
Writer: Wendell Mayes, based on the novel by Paul Gallico

The Poseidon Adventure, which helped create the disaster movie craze of the seventies, assures us that even in a capsized and rapidly sinking ship that's stranded in the middle of a midnight ocean, we can save ourselves—as long as we are willing to climb up a fifty-foot-tall metal tree in a pair of opera pumps to reach the promise of rescue.

At midnight on New Year's Eve, the SS *Poseidon*, a ship already compromised by corporate greed and a strained production budget, is struck by a tidal wave. The world is literally turned upside down as the luxury liner capsizes in the middle of the vast, dark, and unfriendly ocean. Many of the passengers are ready to give up as chandeliers are turned into chaise longues and swimming pools become skylights. But not Reverend Frank Scott (Gene Hackman), who has a pull-yourself-up-by-your-bootstraps, Up-with-People–style spirituality that comes in handy in this world where what once was up is now down and vice versa.

Reverend Frank convinces nine survivors to join him on his journey up to the bottom. His companions on this inverted journey include the usual disaster movie all-star cast: Ernest Borgnine as a tough-talking New York cop, Shelley Winters as a Jewish grandmother on her way to see her grandson in Israel, and Red Buttons and Roddy McDowall are in there somewhere too. Together they defy gravity to get to the rescue boats on the surface.

Watch this movie when you can't tell up from down and need to be rescued, at least for a few hours, from your personal disaster. *The Poseidon Adventure* will remind you that in a world turned topsy-turvy, sometimes you have to do the opposite of what your instincts tell you, and challenge the normal physics of your universe, if you ever hope to save yourself and reach the morning after.

Best Pickup Lines

*I would rather be your best friend than the guy
who made you give up any part of yourself.*

★ William Fichtner as Aaron in *Passion of Mind*

If you want me to stop, tell me now.

★ Clint Eastwood as Robert Kincaid in *The Bridges of Madison County*

You are everything I never knew I always wanted.

★ Matthew Perry as Alex Whitman in *Fools Rush In*

*I love that you get cold when it's seventy-one degrees out. I love
that it takes you an hour and a half to order a sandwich. I
love that you get a little crinkle in your nose when you're looking at me like I'm nuts. I love that after I spend the day with
you, I can still smell your perfume on my clothes. And I love
that you are the last person I want to talk to before I go to
sleep at night.*

★ Billy Crystal as Harry Burns in *When Harry Met Sally*

There's not a part of you that I don't know, remember, and want.

★ Robert Montgomery as Elyot in *Private Lives*

*Come on. We've got a lot to do. I've got to drink to you, you've got
to drink to me, and we've both got to drink to each other.
What do you say—should we start?*

★ Cary Grant as Andre Charville in *Suzy*

■ *Fun with Dick and Jane* (1977)

Stars: Jane Fonda, George Segal
Director: Ted Kotcheff
Writers: Gerald Gaiser, David Giler

In a seventies interpretation of existentialism, *Fun with Dick and Jane* comforts us with the illusion that when ends don't meet, crime does pay, that any behavior is permissible as long as your victim is more corrupt than you are, and that sometimes rescue means never having to say you're sorry—even if you've committed larceny.

Jane Fonda and George Segal star as Dick and Jane Harper, a young couple living the 1970s version of the American dream: big house in the suburbs, two and a half baths, kids, swimming pool being dug in the backyard, and then blammo! George loses his job and their Ivory soap bubble world bursts, leaving them seventy thousand dollars in debt and in danger of losing their home. This makes it very hard to keep up with the Joneses, which shouldn't matter to a spiritual seventies couple who have transcended suburban morality, but somehow along the way, that swimming pool became really important to them.

Rather than risking their membership in the upper-middle-class club, George turns to crime and begins robbing package stores to pay the bills. But poor George isn't much better at grand theft than he was at being an advertising executive, so it's up to his wife to carry off the capers. They metamorphose into a kind of Bonnie and Clyde lite, stealing from the rich to give to the poor, and to make their mortgage payments on time.

When you're in over your head and sinking fast, watch *Fun with Dick and Jane* and remember that sometimes you've got to bend the rules if you want to deliver yourself from the inevitable.

Jane's Jewels

Modeling is just organized walking.
   ★ Jane Fonda as Jane Harper in *Fun with Dick and Jane*

A girl's best friend is her mama. At least, that's what it says on the greeting cards.
   ★ Jane Fonda as Iris in *Stanley and Iris*

■ **The Princess Bride** (1987)
Stars: Robin Wright, Cary Elwes, Billy Crystal, Chris Sarandon
Director: Rob Reiner
Writer: William Goldman, based on his novel

No matter what she asks of him, he replies, "As you wish," and hops to it. Wherever she goes, he follows, even if it requires scaling rocky cliffs hundreds of feet high, enduring torture in the pit of despair, and wrestling with "rodents of an unusual size." Our hero, Westley (Cary Elwes), is not only a self-sacrificing gentleman but a master of acrobatic swordplay, which he engages in while dressed in all black, a head scarf, and a leather eye mask—kind of a cross between Don Juan, Zorro, and Miami Steve Van Zandt. Hmm . . . if this flick weren't rated PG, we'd love to see what other commands of hers he would so willingly obey.

Anyway, in this fairy tale, there are plenty of giants and castles and mugging moments by character actors like Billy Crystal, but at its heart it's the story of a wronged princess (Robin Wright) who manages to rise above her sappy name (Buttercup) and stand up to the evil prince who wishes to destroy her happiness (Chris Sarandon). Still, even a self-actualized and grounded princess can appreciate being shadowed by a dashing young admirer determined to rise from the dead if necessary to serve her. Watch *The Princess Bride* when he's been less than considerate of late and remember, you don't have to become kidnapped by pirates to be worthy of the attentions of a brave and chivalrous fellow in a leather mask.

■ **That Touch of Mink** (1962)
Stars: Doris Day, Cary Grant
Director: Delbert Mann
Writers: Stanley Shapiro, Nate Monaster

That Touch of Mink is one of those Hollywood-style escapist confections that manages to defy all the principles of emotional and psychological gravity, floating our couple up to seventh heaven on a silver-lined cloud of love, despite the fact that they are way over the excess baggage limit.

Cathy Timberlake (Doris Day) is a simple country girl transplanted to the big bad city to seek her fame and fortune. Despite a working-girl pluckiness that just seems to come naturally to her, and a couple of very convincing Chanel knockoffs, Cathy is really just an old-fashioned girl at heart, with old-fashioned dreams, old-fashioned hang-ups, and an old-fashioned temper when it comes to getting splashed with mud by the Rolls-Royces of thoughtless international playboys.

Enter Philip Shayne (Cary Grant), a debonair (when *isn't* Cary debonair?), martini-drinking, Rolls-Royce–driving chief executive of a multinational corporation who is really just a family man at heart. Despite his bevy of bikini-clad heiresses awaiting his arrival in every port, and his standing reservation in the honeymoon suite at the Ritz Côte d'Azur, he's really just been pining for a hometown gal like Cathy to convince him to retire his shaker and settle down. Yeah, right.

Despite the epic denial going on in this movie, or perhaps because of it, this is a great flick to watch when you need to be rescued from reality. So pop it in the VCR, take wing over a Mediterranean sea of dysfunction, and fly far far away.

> ⚠ Warning Label: *Do not drive or operate heavy machinery while under the influence of this medication. Denial and drill presses are not a good combo.*

■ *Love on the Run* (1936)
Stars: Clark Gable, Joan Crawford, Franchot Tone, Reginald Owen
Director: W. S. Van Dyke
Writers: John Lee Mahin, Manuel Seff, Gladys Hurlbut,
*   from a story by Alan Green and Julian Brodie*

Sally Parker (Joan Crawford) just wants to get away from her mercenary ex-fiancé (a Russian baron) and the pressure of notoriety—you know how everyone just hounds nice society gals. It's so very tiring, when all one wants to do is don yet another fabulous gown by Adrian, sigh over one's misfortunes, and have tea on the porch. So when a friendly stranger named Michael Anthony (Clark Gable) shows up out of nowhere, she immediately jumps into the nearest propeller plane with him and heads overseas, no questions asked.

Well, of course, Sally runs into more trouble than she bargained for. That awful Michael is secretly a reporter, sending dispatches to the *New York Chronicle* about their adventures in the countryside of France. Meanwhile poor Sally is stuck wearing a borrowed gossamer white sequined gown, forced to sleep in some silk-sheeted queen's bed in a French museum, and kidnapped by a gentleman spy who insists that she don his wife's mink-and-velvet ensemble and dine with him at an haute cuisine restaurant. Don't you just hate when that happens? And somehow, it's all Michael's fault, the cad!

In the mood to lose yourself in a far more glamorous set of problems than your own? Join Gable and Crawford in this frolic and pretend that even when you spend the night in a cart filled with pigs and cabbages, you will wake up with perfect lipstick, the perfect man, and not a false eyelash out of place.

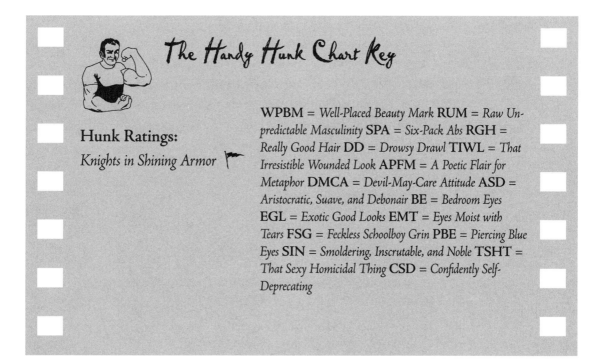

The Handy Hunk Chart Key

Hunk Ratings:

Knights in Shining Armor ⚑

WPBM = *Well-Placed Beauty Mark* **RUM** = *Raw Unpredictable Masculinity* **SPA** = *Six-Pack Abs* **RGH** = *Really Good Hair* **DD** = *Drowsy Drawl* **TIWL** = *That Irresistible Wounded Look* **APFM** = *A Poetic Flair for Metaphor* **DMCA** = *Devil-May-Care Attitude* **ASD** = *Aristocratic, Suave, and Debonair* **BE** = *Bedroom Eyes* **EGL** = *Exotic Good Looks* **EMT** = *Eyes Moist with Tears* **FSG** = *Feckless Schoolboy Grin* **PBE** = *Piercing Blue Eyes* **SIN** = *Smoldering, Inscrutable, and Noble* **TSHT** = *That Sexy Homicidal Thing* **CSD** = *Confidently Self-Deprecating*

The Handy Hunk Chart

William Powell   ASD, CSD, DMCA

Top Drool Pics: *How to Marry a Millionaire,* the *Thin Man* series, *Life with Father, The Great Ziegfeld, The Ziegfeld Follies, Love Crazy, I Love You Again, Libeled Lady, My Man Godfrey, Reckless, Manhattan Melodrama*

Before motorcycle jackets made the man, before having severe intimacy issues traceable to a fractured father relationship made a guy hot stuff, before punching out paparazzi made an actor seem all the more desirable, there was William Powell, a man who was born in a tux. A man who knew that a lady deserves to be treated like a lady even when she's behaving like a spoiled brat (hey, we all have our days). A man who knew that a martini is shaken, never stirred. A man who had full command of the rules of grammar and never slipped on the subjunctive. A man who defined unflappable, who could weather with grace any storm and emerge pressed, impeccably groomed, and ready with a strong arm. And yet while William Powell was all of these things, he also had that playful, dimpled grin and a boyish charm that shone through the veneer of a perfect gentleman. Mr. Powell, you can pop our ornaments anytime. ■

Will Smith   ASD, BE, RGH, CSD, DMCA, FSG

Top Drool Pics: *Men in Black, The Legend of Bagger Vance, Independence Day, Six Degrees of Separation, Enemy of the State*

Face it—Will Smith's long, lean, muscular-machine bod is the reason they make fine Italian suits. We bet there are millions of sheep the world over who are begging to be sheared just for the honor of draping Will in

. . . *continued*

gabardine. And yet for all his dignity, poise, and long-limbed grace, for all the 100 percent Colombian mountain grown richness of his voice, he's got that wonderful deadpan wit and mischievousness that reassures us that Will walks among us. He has managed to create the screen image of the ultimate modern man who is deeply attracted to his strong-willed wife and who negatively compares a lingerie model to his own woman at home (yeah, right). And in *Independence Day*, Will even managed to make shameless American jingoism look sexy.

Okay, so his sugar jar ears that rival Clark Gable's can get distracting at times, but they give him an air of boyishness that makes him seem all the more accessible. So we'll just pretend for a couple of hours that Will is our very own and savor his unique blend of playfulness and passion, even if it means sitting through some damn golf movie. ■

■ ***The Sound of Music*** *(1965)*
Stars: Julie Andrews, Christopher Plummer
Director: Robert Wise
Writers: Richard Rodgers, Oscar Hammerstein II

"How do you solve a problem like Maria?" Well, you could fix her up with a wealthy widower who has a built-in family and a luxurious home with a delightful gazebo, not to mention a lovely tenor voice that will harmonize perfectly with hers when they are clutching each other by moonlight and crooning Rodgers and Hammerstein tunes about their misspent youth. Throw in a little heart-stirring intrigue in the form of an approaching Nazi army, and a daring escape across the Alps, and you've got the perfect rescue fantasy.

We've got to admire Maria's (Julie Andrews) spunk—she's not afraid to speak up to the rigid Captain von Trapp (Christopher Plummer) or psychologically outmaneuver his kids, to whom she plays governess. But everything comes just a little too easily for her, doesn't it? She's a novitiate nun blessed with a mother superior who knows the perfect cure for her internal confusion, an employer who falls madly in love with her the first time he waltzes with her, a group of hostile brats that are won over by her in twenty-four hours, a dysfunctional family dynamic that gets cured in one harmonized chorus, and a rival for the captain's affections who is eliminated from the competition in one game of four square with the kids.

And can we talk about those draperies in Maria's room that are large enough for her to outfit seven children in hideous green-flowered lederhosen and dirndls? Just how long did it take Maria to design, measure, cut, and sew those monstrosities? Did she work on them in her free time after the kids went to sleep? Did she ever get compensated for all that overtime?

Ah, somehow, when we watch that spirited frolicking in the mountain meadows to the tune of "Do Re Mi," reality feels as far away as the threat of fascism. Watch *The Sound of Music* when you are feeling out of tune with the world and you'll find yourself believing that your problems will be solved in a jiffy if you just put a little spring in your step and a merry song in your heart.

▪ *Thrill of a Romance* (1945)
Stars: Esther Williams, Van Johnson, Carleton Young
Director: Richard Thorpe
Writers: Richard Connell, Gladys Lehman

Cynthia (Esther Williams) deserves to be swept away by a good-looking and rich man, but how is she to guess that her wonderful new beau, Bob Delbar (Carleton Young), isn't a genuine Romeo but a slick egotist who just sees her as a potential trophy wife? Well, Cynthia, we'll let you in on a secret: guys who ask you out because they see you in a bathing suit, then messenger over a copy of *Fortune* magazine so you can read the puff piece on them, and have a PI check out your background before they ask you to dinner, are generally not good husband material.

Luckily Major Thomas Milvaine (Van Johnson) discovers Cynthia at a luxury hotel in Beverly Hills and devotes himself to discovering what is causing that glycerine tear to roll down her cheek, and to healing her wounded feminine heart. And while Major Milvaine soothes her with all the gentleness of a rosewater bath, our gal just keeps showing up in one fabulous gown after another as Tommy Dorsey and his band play, an opera singer bursts into song again and again, and even the bellboy opens his mouth to let loose a show-stopping, heart-wrenching torch song to distract her from her sorrows.

Everything here has the thin veneer of Hollywood gloss, from the overlit, oil-painted backdrops to Esther's makeup, which remains perfect no matter how many back dives she performs. But that's the fun of this movie. It's got kitschy pool scenes, cornball secondary characters, endless musical numbers, costumes that make you wonder how many suitcases one woman can possibly travel with, and the perfect romance. Indulge in this flick when you're in need of a frothy one with a little pink umbrella and a coconut cup. Yummy!

Worst Pickup Lines

Now listen, sweet meat, how 'bout you and me getting together tonight?

    ★ Clark Gable to Jean Harlow in *Hold Your Man*

I've known you in every ripple of moonlight I've ever seen and every symphony I've ever heard, and every perfume I've ever smelled . . . your hair, your hair is like a field of silver daisies. I'd like to run barefoot through your hair.

    ★ Franchot Tone as Gifford Middleton in *Bombshell*

It's not even my dick anymore. It's attached to me, yeah, but it belongs to you. I'll take it a step further: I'm telling you that not only at this point with you, because I'm so attached to you, is every other girl on earth not exciting to me in the slightest, every other girl on earth to me, it's like a salamander—it's like something that came from under a fucking rock. It's disgusting to me.

    ★ Robert Downey, Jr., as Blake in *Two Girls and a Guy*

Meet me in the bedroom in five minutes and bring a cattle prod.

    ★ Tatsuya Mihashi as Phil Moskowitz in *What's Up, Tiger Lily?*

▪ *Double Jeopardy* (1999)
Stars: Ashley Judd, Tommy Lee Jones
Director: Bruce Beresford
Writers: David Weisberg, Douglas Cook

Libby Parsons (Ashley Judd) has it all. She's the young, rich, and beautiful wife of a young, rich, and beautiful man, with a young, rich, and beautiful son, and even a boat, which, of course, is also beautiful. And expensive.

Of course, as we all know, this kind of perfection presented in the first two minutes of any film is always a setup for total and complete devastation. And sure enough, next thing we know, chaos knocks at the solid-oak-with-period-molding cabin door. On an overnight getaway sail with her husband, Libby awakes to find the sails torn, the pristine poop deck mucked up with blood (which stains, you know), and her husband gone. Next thing you know, the cherubic son is farmed out for adoption and young, beautiful, and rich Libby Parsons, wrongfully convicted of her husband's murder, becomes a penniless—albeit still young and beautiful—jailbird.

Enter Travis Lehman (Tommy Lee Jones), Libby's embittered, by-the-book parole officer with a heart of gold whose draconian discipline does nothing to stop Libby from pursuing the justice she deserves.

And, because this is a justice-prevails movie, the husband gets it—in spades. The rest of the movie is an all-you-can-eat revenge buffet. In the end, everybody gets everything he deserves and then some. What a refreshing treat when you feel like the world's punching bag, and how reassuring to remember that when the knights in shining armor are on strike, we can rescue ourselves.

▪ *Easy Living* (1937)
Stars: Jean Arthur, Edward Arnold, Ray Milland, Mary Nash
Director: Mitchell Leisen
Writer: Preston Sturges, based on the play by Vera Caspary

Mary Smith (Jean Arthur) hasn't got enough nickels in her piggy bank to buy herself a beef pie at the Automat, but life, she soon learns, is as unpredictable as a dot-com's fortunes. In this Depression-era comedy, a clever, forthright, sweet, and hardworking everywoman watches her luck turn, starting when a sable coat drops on her head. Next she meets John Ball, Jr. (Ray Milland), at the Automat. He's a fella with a kind heart and a key to the kitchen, but they aren't eating vending machine food for long. In one of those completely absurd screwball comedy plots, Mary and John end up moving into a mind-bogglingly luxurious hotel suite together, all expenses paid by the owner. And then John turns out not to be a pauper after all but a well-diversified prince who makes the Rockefellers, Mellons, and Carnegies look like social climbers. Yes, by the third act, he's been taken back in by his wealthy father (Edward Arnold) and mother (Mary Nash), who has enough fur coats in her closet to render an entire species extinct. And naturally, John is ready to pop the question to Mary, who will never have to consume low-grade beef products again.

If you're feeling disheartened by your financial fortunes lately, why not take a trip to a world where shopgirls end up as millionaires?

Chapter 4

"It's a Guy Thing": Understanding Your Man Movies

Where did he get the idea that intimacy is a four-letter word? Why can't he understand that football is not the only metaphor for life? How can you convince him that commitment is not a skin rash, and why can't he get it through his thick head that asking for directions is not an indication of fundamental gender confusion?

Let's face it. Guys are . . . well . . . they're a mystery, and trying to puzzle out what's going on in those thick heads of theirs can give us all an emotional migraine. Fortunately, we have the movies to help us see the world through our guy's eyes and understand the method behind his madness.

So if you're having trouble getting a handle on what makes your man tick, watch one of these Understanding Your Man Movies guaranteed to cure your "can't live with 'em, can't shoot 'em" blues, and give you the clues you'll need to solve the mystery of the opposite sex.

■ *Taxi Driver* (1976)
Stars: *Robert De Niro, Jodie Foster, Harvey Keitel, Cybill Shepherd*
Director: *Martin Scorsese*
Writer: *Paul Schrader*

Taxi Driver is a classic example of the weird love affair that guys have with cinematic down-and-outers. There is something about a disenfranchised and iconoclastic underdog who drops out of life, shaves his head, purchases a weapon on the black market, and starts boning up on his assassination skills that just makes a guy's heart go pitter-pat.

In this seminal addition to the scum-must-go genre, Travis Bickle (Robert De Niro) is an alienated, anonymous, and insomniac Vietnam vet who drives a cab through the gritty midnight streets of Manhattan in search of his place in the world. As he drives, Travis interacts with the primordial ooze of the New York swamp, including a ponytailed pimp called Sport (Harvey Keitel) and Iris the teenage prostitute (a barely pubescent Jodie Foster).

This nightly interaction with the dark heart of the city fuels Travis's obsessive notion that he has a divine calling to rid New York of its filth. In a classic example of the delusions of heroic grandeur typical of the genre, Travis imagines himself as a great rain that will fall onto the city like righteous vengeance, and wash the streets clean.

Okay, so we get the whole thing about wanting to clean up city streets, but you know, Travis, they have street sweepers and alternate-side parking that can accomplish the very same thing without the use of duct tape, eighties-inspired club warrior dos, or contraband munitions. And as anyone who has ever been in New York City during a garbage strike knows, it takes a village to keep the sidewalks clean. But the limitations of the physical universe don't stop Travis because he is a man with a mission, an updated Don Quixote tilting at windmills in a futile attempt to recapture his own innocence.

Watch this movie when your disenfranchised iconoclast has locked himself in the dingy inner-city hotel room of his subconscious, and has started shouting, "You talkin' to me?" *Taxi Driver* will help you to understand that inside every disenfranchised drifter is the heart of an impassioned priest in search of a new faith. Although, if he asks you out on a date, it's probably a good idea if you pick the movie . . . and don't let him near a barbershop until he's in a better frame of mind.

World-Class Loser Lines

*You talkin' to me? You talkin' to me? You talkin' to
me? Then who the hell else are you talkin' to? You
talkin' to me? Well, I'm the only one here. Who do
you think you're talking to? Oh, yeah? Huh? Okay.*

★ Robert De Niro as Travis Bickle in *Taxi Driver*

■ *The Insider* (1999)
Stars: Russell Crowe, Al Pacino, Christopher Plummer
Director: Michael Mann
Writer: Marie Brenner, based on an article by Eric Roth

The usual Hollywood hero doesn't wear glasses or work out his frustrations by hitting a few golf balls around, and his middle isn't quite as thick as Russell Crowe's is here (okay, we make an exception for Clark Gable in his bloated later years). But *The Insider* proves that a fellow doesn't have to have fantastic upper-body development or the ability to hang from helicopters while shooting at bad guys to stir our hearts.

Russell Crowe plays Jeffrey Wigand, a real-life whistle-blower who risked and lost all in order to expose the lies of big tobacco companies. As we see him grimly set his chubby jaw and nervously adjust his glasses, we don't think of Dilbert so much as a modern-day gladiator going up against the entire Roman Empire. Hmm, now there's an idea for a guy movie.

But back to *The Insider*. We won't venture to guess why in real life Wigand's wife chose not to stand by her man, but we can say this about her fictional counterpart: maybe she wasn't so upset by her husband exposing her and the kids to danger as she was by his steadfast refusal to discuss it with her beforehand. Yes, if only this were a Frank Capra movie—Wigand would've launched into a filibuster in order to force folks to do the right thing and his Donna Reed-esque wife would look up at him in loving support. And then there would've been a chorus of "Auld Lang Syne." And some bells would've rung. But in real life, some men are better at being heroes and saving the world than being communicators and saving their marriages.

Watch this when your own strong and silent type is driving you nuts; maybe it'll help you to see a nobility behind his stoicism.

Reel to Real

The real-life Jeffrey Wigand asked the filmmakers for two things: that they change the names of his daughters and that they not have any character in the film shown smoking.

Them's Fightin' Words

Agent: Do you have a history of emotional problems, Mr. Wigand?

Jeffrey Wigand (Russell Crowe): Yes. Yes, I do. I get extremely emotional when assholes put bullets in my mailbox!

Heavy Metal: Male Rivalry Movies

Pissing contests go back to prehistoric days and will probably be with us for as long as the sky stays blue and guys harbor masculinity issues. In ancient times, men would simply club one another over the head with a blunt object and be done with it. Whoever didn't lose consciousness got the girl and the

. . . continued

best cave on the block. In the Iron Age guys figured out how to forge spears and things got a little uglier. Today guys have found a less corporeal approach to competition. Today they joust with tin.

Pushing Tin (1999)
Stars: John Cusack, Billy Bob Thornton, Angelina Jolie, Cate Blanchett
Director: Mike Newell
Writers: Darcy Frey, Glen Charles

Air traffic control, or "pushing tin," is a metaphor for masculinity in this male rivalry movie about two air traffic controllers who go head-to-head, using jumbo jets and their wives as props in a duel to the death to prove who is the most macho.

Nick "The Zone" Falzone (John Cusack), the undisputed tin-pushing king of the skies in the fast-paced fly zone above New York City, finds his reign threatened by the entrance of a cowboy controller called Russell Bell (Billy Bob Thornton). Russell out-studs Nick at every turn, and even wears a feather stuck into his headset while he works because he's half Indian, which is way more exotic and cool than The Zone has ever been. And to make matters worse, he beats Nick at Ping-Pong—every single time. What ensues is a relentless metaphorical pissing contest, with Nick pushing the limits of his emotional and psychological fly space in an attempt to write his name in the sky bigger than Bell can.

This movie gives us gals a great refresher course in the dos and don'ts of macho. Much of it we knew already—for instance, that guys do stuff like kick over motorcycles and expose their fingers to the flame just to prove how tough they are. But there are a few surprises. For example, Ping-Pong and "Muskrat Love" are both macho. So are select ballads by Bread, and being sensitive to your wife's needs—now, there's a stretch.

Watch this movie when your macho man is pushing his tin around and courting a midair collision. Maybe he'll learn, like Nick does, that the measure

. . . *continued*

of a man is not how long he can hold on to a lit match in a chicken contest, but how successfully he loves himself, and his wife and children.

Tin Men (1987)
Stars: Richard Dreyfuss, Danny DeVito, Barbara Hershey
Director and Writer: Barry Levinson

Cadillacs are a metaphor for masculinity in this male rivalry movie about two aluminum siding salesmen, or "tin men," who go head-to-head, using aluminum siding, their Cadillacs, and their wives as props in a duel to the death to prove who is the most macho. Sound familiar?

Bill "BB" Babowsky (Richard Dreyfuss), a king in the aluminum siding world, backs his brand-new Caddy out of the showroom right into the path of his competitor Ernest Tilley's (Danny DeVito) Cadillac. When phallic symbols collide, these two outlaws of the suburban frontier engage in a no-holds-barred contest to resurrect the dented fenders of their manhood.

Watch this one when your suburban outlaw is flexing his fenders, and remind yourselves that the measure of a man is not the size of his sedan but the tenderness in his tank.

■ Animal House (1978)
Stars: John Belushi, Peter Riegert, Tim Matheson, Karen Allen,
Tom Hulce, John Vernon
Director: John Landis
Writers: Douglas Kenney, Harold Ramis

Delta House is a college frat house circa 1962 that reflects the attitudes of the golden age of politically incorrect movies, making light of things like date rape and college kids drinking until they hurl. Mostly, though, this is a movie about how really, really stupid guys can be when they're all together in the same house without the civilizing influence of a woman.

Delta is so disreputable that they'll take just about anybody who pledges as long as they understand that partying is the first priority of college life. Members include such luminary young scions of society as Bluto (John Belushi), whose most notable accomplishments in seven years of higher education are learning that the Germans bombed Pearl Harbor and sticking french fries really far up his nose. And then there's Boon (Peter Riegert), our leading man, who would rather dress up in a bedsheet and pour booze over his head than settle down with his sensible college sweetheart and get a life.

Trouble brews when Dean Wormer (John Vernon), a tweed-and-bow-tie-wearing metaphor for blind authority, declares that the next time the Deltas screw up, every Animal House brother will be expelled. Dean Wormer enlists the assistance of a psychotic ROTC recruit called Neidermeyer (Mark Metcalf), and Omega House, a rival frat whose members are characterized by good behavior, bad haircuts, and letter sweaters, to harass the Deltas off campus. Not surprisingly, the Delta response to this is to throw a big toga party and get really, really toasted. In the end, though, everyone is forced to recognize that Animal Houses everywhere add a necessary element of masculine high spirits and just the right degree of chaos to keep us honest, and must be celebrated rather than expunged. And of course, boys will be boys.

Okay, so plotwise this movie is not exactly rich with subtlety and nuance, but it's not examining a subtle phenomenon. This is a movie about unbridled adolescent guydom. It's a movie about eating and drinking and nailing chicks and blowing chunks, and about how beneath the sensible, civilized blue suit of adulthood, most guys are still Delta brothers at heart, dying to put on a toga and buck the system. And maybe this isn't such a bad thing.

Watch *Animal House* with your animal when he's refusing to be tamed and remember, without that wild and playful frat boy within, we'd all be married to a bunch of boring Omegas who make hospital corners with their bedsheets, instead of wearing them.

Stupid Guy Quotes

Boon (Peter Riegert): My advice to you is to start drinking heavily.
Bluto (John Belushi): Better listen to him, Flounder. He's premed.

from *Animal House*

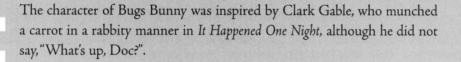

Nancy's Momentous Minutiae: Male Archetypes

The character of James Bond, created by author Ian Fleming, was inspired by debonair Cary Grant—who later turned down the role in the movies.

The character of Bugs Bunny was inspired by Clark Gable, who munched a carrot in a rabbity manner in *It Happened One Night*, although he did not say, "What's up, Doc?".

▪ *True West* (1983)
Stars: John Malkovich, Gary Sinise
Directors: Allan A. Goldstein, Gary Sinise
Writer: Sam Shepard

True West is a cinematic temper tantrum that reminds us that inside every grown man is a terrible toddler who is willing to pull every pot out of every cabinet in the kitchen, smash the typewriter with a five iron, set fire to the toaster, and ruin a perfectly good set of golf clubs to get what he wants, particularly if his brother has got one already.

Austin (Gary Sinise), a struggling screenwriter on the verge of a big deal, is house-sitting his mother's plants when his pugilistic prodigal brother Lee (John Malkovich) pops by for a visit. The ill will that exists between these two brothers is palpable from the moment Lee enters the room and asks to borrow the keys to Austin's car so that he can rob the neighborhood. The tension escalates when Lee, an uneducated drifter living in self-imposed exile in the desert, steals Austin's screenwriting deal right out from under him. In a bizarre turn of the tables, the brothers become each other, experiencing firsthand how green the grass really is on the other side of the fence.

Once they are forced to collaborate, the G-force of their sibling rivalry and their creative process reduces the kitchen, most of the household appliances, and their respective egos to rubble, and in the end they both go away empty-handed. Malkovich and Sinise give body and voice to the male superego, which shouts and drinks and smashes and ignites the world in a bonfire of misdirected energy, and all because they are competing for an absent father's love. Watch this one when the prodigal son in your life is holding his breath until he turns blue. After watching this cardiovascular movie, he'll be gasping for air.

> ⚠ Warning Label: *If he's in one of "those" moods while you're watching this movie, or if his brother is in town, lock up the golf clubs and hide the toaster.*

Smart Guy Quotes

Never joke about a woman's hair, clothes, or menstrual cycle. Page one.

★ John Hannah as James in *Sliding Doors*

Period Peace Pics That Are Actually Gore-Fests and Really Piss Us Off

The Patriot (2000)
Stars: Mel Gibson, Heath Ledger, Joely Richardson
Director: Roland Emmerich
Writer: Robert Rodat

Mel "Family Values" Gibson stars as Revolutionary War hero Benjamin Martin, aka "The Ghost," who vows to remain a pacifist following a bloody career as an officer in the French and Indian War. Horrified by the scale of

. . . continued

his own inner violence, Ben trades his saber for a spade and retires with his family to a bucolic setting reminiscent of a colonial Walton's Mountain. Even when the British are coming, and the whole town pleads with him to lead the troops into battle for American independence, Ben resolutely refuses to put down his shovel and take up arms.

Unfortunately, Ben's son Gabriel (Heath Ledger), the John Boy of the movie, only without the birthmark and with better hair, gets caught up in the nationalist frenzy of the moment and joins the army. In order to protect his son, Ben must pick up his musket once again and begin goring people to death in an operatic orgy of gratuitous bloodletting, all committed in the name of freedom, family, and box office.

Lame Excuses

I'm a parent. I haven't got the luxury of principles.
★ Mel Gibson as Benjamin Martin in *The Patriot*

Now this might have been a successful conclusion from a military perspective, and it certainly seems to have paid off in box office receipts, but it's an emotional and psychological disaster. Rather than learning from experience, Ben decides to repeat his bloody mistakes—only this time, he does it in front of his children. Actually, he does it in front of *all* of our children and winds up with two dead sons, a dead daughter-in-law, a farm burned to the ground, a five-year-old who is a hysterical mute, and a lifetime of regret. But hey, he did make some really good war buddies in the process.

. . . *continued*

Gladiator (2000)
Stars: *Russell Crowe, Joaquin Phoenix, Connie Nielsen*
Director: *Ridley Scott*
Writers: *David Franzoni, John Logan, William Nicholson*

Gladiator has turned American movie houses, and now our living rooms, into the Roman Colosseum, where well-muscled heroes with cudgels in their hands hack each other to bits as we decadent citizens of a crumbling empire look on with a bag of pork rinds in our hand, and cheer.

Russell Crowe stars as Maximus, a general of the armies of the north, who rains hell on his enemies but is loved and worshiped by his soldiers, mostly because he has this really soft, fatherly voice. He runs afoul of the empire when aging Emperor Marcus Aurelius chooses Maximus over his own son Commodus (Joaquin Phoenix) to rule Rome after he is gone because Maximus is just more of a stand-up guy.

Yeah, right, the good guy gets the throne . . . like *that's* gonna happen. This is Roman history after all, and eventually, a classical revenge tragedy set up like this is going to get ugly. And sure enough, it does. Much Byzantine violence ensues, as well as a couple of semi-incestuous love scenes, and a rousing and poignant conclusion featuring lots of chariots.

On the positive side, *Gladiator* cautions dads everywhere to pay more attention to their daughters and sons, lest they wind up precipitating the fall of Rome in a misguided bid for paternal approval. On the negative side this is an opulent, big-screen, megabudget gore-fest about how many heads you can hoist on one petard and still avoid an NC-17 rating.

Lame Excuses

I am required to kill, so I kill. That is enough.
★   Russell Crowe as Maximus in *Gladiator*

■ *Goodfellas* (1990)
Stars: Robert De Niro, Ray Liotta, Joe Pesci, Lorraine Bracco
Director: Martin Scorsese
Writers: Nicholas Pileggi, Martin Scorsese

This is a movie about how somewhere deep down in a small and often overlooked part of themselves, a lot of men are really turned on by the fantasy of becoming a sociopathic wiseguy just like Henry Hill (Ray Liotta). They're aching to dress in two-thousand-dollar Italian suits and have a reserved table in every nightclub and a witness protection program waiting for them when their tailor bills finally come due. Henry Hill's story is the ultimate male fantasy. He's a man who is able to exist above the law, and behave as badly as he wants to, until the law catches up with him.

Henry Hill is an Irish Italian American kid from the mean streets of New York's Lower East Side. Henry grows up admiring the well-dressed men of respect in the neighborhood, and dreams of one day becoming just like them. And just like in all of our beloved morality tales about self-made second-generation Americans who capture their slice of the grand dream, all of Henry's wishes come true.

Henry becomes a heartless and homicidal gangster as well as a drug addict and an unfaithful husband. But he does dress really, really well, and he gets front-row-center tables at Frank Sinatra concerts. And he makes a great jailhouse marinara sauce. And he's got this really creepy, hollow, joyless laugh that really unnerves people and is cool to pull out at parties because it freaks everybody out.

Watch *Goodfellas* with your wise guy and let him know that you love him just the way he is, even without the cool threads and the hot tickets.

■ *The Man in the Gray Flannel Suit* (1956)
Stars: Gregory Peck, Jennifer Jones
Director: Nunnally Johnson
Writer: Nunnally Johnson, based on the novel by Sloan Wilson

Assigned by a would-be employer to write an essay on "the most significant thing about me," Tom Rath (Gregory Peck)—who fathered a child out of wedlock by an Italian girl during World War II, killed seventeen men face-to-face in battle, and is increasingly estranged from his wife and kids—can come up with nothing more interesting or revealing than "I am interested in working for your company." Hardly a sales pitch designed to appeal to the heart, but in 1955, the ability to hold your emotional cards to your chest was greatly valued, so of course Tom, the man in the gray flannel suit, nails the position.

His wife (Jennifer Jones) is thrilled with his new better-paying job because she's feeling claustrophobic in their starter home (although frankly, we think she ought to consider that the limitations of the space she inhabits are less a literal problem than a figurative one). But within weeks, this middle management position has Tom in a political pickle. To make matters worse, his home and finances are threatened by someone challenging his grandmother's will, and he's got to break it to his wife that somewhere in Rome there's a tousle-haired youth who looks just like him. No wonder he's knocking back a scotch and water every night at 5:30.

Now it's true that the-man-in-the-gray-flannel-suit's particular dilemmas have changed over the years. It's a little easier to understand why that postwar generation of men tended to swallow their difficult feelings when you think about what they lived through on the front than it is to understand impenetrable stoicism on the part of today's men. You'd think guys who have Loggins and Messina records in their record collection, a forgotten can of mousse under the sink, or *Iron John* on their bookshelves would be long over that repress-your-feelings-and-have-another-highball garbage, but the fact is that like martinis, wingtips, and cigars, repression of the yin within is back in fashion for guys. What's a gal to do but sigh, urge him to keep an eye on his blood pressure, and wait for a new zeitgeist?

Meanwhile, if your fellow is acting emotionally constipated and blaming it on the difficulty of switching out of his workplace self, watch this movie and we bet you'll feel a little more empathy for him.

Bev's Culinarytherapy: Food for Every Mood

When-You're-Trying-to-Get-in-Touch-with-Your-Inner-Guy Food

When you're getting in touch with your inner average joe—you know, the self that lets the dishes pile up while it takes in some prime entertainment and consumes megaportions of carbs, fats, and sugars—whip up one of these couch potato favorites, and then sit back and watch your belly bloat.

Hot Dog Enchiladas

1 package foot-long hot dogs (full fat, full sodium, no poultry or tofu!)

1 package white-flour tortillas (burrito size, made with lard and hydrogenated vegetable oils)

1 can enchilada sauce

1 bag Monterey Jack cheese (pregrated, full fat)

Poke a hole in the hot dog package and microwave them until they blow up real good. Sprinkle cheese and enchilada sauce on a tortilla and nuke it until the cheese melts, then roll the dog in the tortilla and eat it in three mouthfuls. Chase it with a beer, even if the sun isn't past the yardarm yet. You can mow the lawn tomorrow.

Bologna Boats

Place American cheese on slices of bologna and broil until the bologna curls. Serve promptly with crackers.

. . . continued

Cheese Breeze

Mix cheddar cheese and crumbled cooked bacon. Spread on toast and broil. Serve promptly.

Tiny Broiled Sausages

Broil a lot of very small sausages. Serve with very small buns.

■ *Galaxy Quest* (1999)
Stars: *Tim Allen, Alan Rickman, Sigourney Weaver, Tony Shalhoub, Enrico Colantoni*
Director: *Dean Parisot*
Writers: *David Howard, Robert Gordon*

What is it about guys and their Walter Mitty fantasies? Why do they feel they've gotta go out there and fight archetypal battles of good versus evil in order to be proud of themselves? Somehow the simple heroism of showing up on time and doing your job just doesn't cut it for them, which explains why hordes of young men spend so much time in an alternative reality known as a sci-fi convention. Yeah, okay, there are some women there too, but the plotlines of most of those sci-fi television shows are really designed to push the emotional hot buttons of the boys who just wanna pretend they're fighting for truth, justice, and the humanoid way. If you've ever wondered just what would make a guy who isn't interested in going to a weekend workshop on relationship communication skills spend a week taking a Klingon-immersion course, *Galaxy Quest* will enlighten you.

In this spoof of Trekkies, Tim Allen plays Jason Nesmith, an aging, egotistical, would-be playboy actor who is still cashing in on his performance as starship captain in a beloved, if long since canceled, low-budget sci-fi TV series called *Galaxy Quest*. He and his fellow actors (Sigourney Weaver, Alan Rickman, and Tony Shalhoub) get caught up in the real-life struggles of a race of guileless aliens who don't understand artifice and think that the TV shows they've been watching are historical documents. Suddenly, the ex-Questers are facing death at the claws of a large, green, lizardlike monster. Will the Questers live up to the hero-worship of these woefully misinformed fellow Milky Way–ites—and live long enough to make it to the next *Galaxy Quest* convention?

It's true that the more you know about *Star Trek*, the more you'll love this flick, but it's a great movie to watch whenever you're exasperated with trying to figure out why your fella insists on pretending he's something he's not. *Galaxy Quest* will help you see that a guy will get in way over his head because he wants so badly to be admired as a hero by someone—even if it is a gullible creature from another planet.

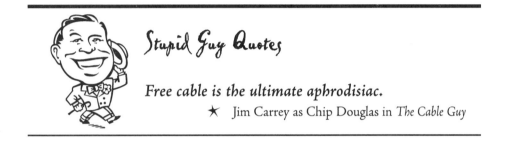

Stupid Guy Quotes

Free cable is the ultimate aphrodisiac.

★ Jim Carrey as Chip Douglas in *The Cable Guy*

■ *Wayne's World* (1992)

Stars: Mike Myers, Dana Carvey, Rob Lowe, Tia Carrere
Director: Penelope Spheeris
Writers: Mike Myers, Bonnie Turner, Terry Turner

Wayne's World is a crash course in male perennial adolescence, and reminds us all that no matter how polished, cool, and together a guy might appear to be on the surface, somewhere, way down deep, he feels a lot like a cable geek in a basement who lucked into a network deal that's just a little bit over his head.

The plot of this movie is, much like the best-laid plans of its main characters, completely circuitous and rather beside the point. Basically, a slick and creatively insensitive ad exec (Rob Lowe) spots Wayne and Garth's cable access program *Wayne's World* and takes it to the big time. Benjamin tricks Wayne (Mike Myers) and Garth (Dana Carvey) into selling their program outright for peanuts, and then sells out the soul of the show to satisfy the sponsor. Oh, and Ben also tries to steal Wayne's girlfriend, Cassandra (Tia Carrere), a singer with a rock-and-roll soul and legs for days who is also able to throw a really mean roundhouse kick while wearing stiletto-heeled stage boots.

That last image should have tipped you off to the fact that what this movie is really about is the presentation of a meticulously constructed adolescent male Shangri-la, containing all of the landmark icons in the fantasy life of guys, including stiletto-heeled stage boots. In this never-never land, guys get to buy the pre-CBS Fender Stratocaster for cash, and nail the great-looking babe even though their career objective is to acquire an expansive collection of name tags and hair nets, and they still live with their parents. Yes, it's a teenage utopia; everything from drug overdoses to a sexual identity crisis can be solved with an implausible sci-fi solution and generous quantities of coffee and cruller. And most important of all, no matter what pressures come to bear on our heroes from the outside world, nothing in Wayne and Garth's more perfect basement ever, ever changes.

According to *Wayne's World*, when you get right down to the basement of things, what makes guys happy is the same thing that makes us gals happy: good creative work, good creative fun, and a whole lot of good creative loving. It's just, in a guy's perfect world, the furniture doesn't get rearranged very often.

Wayne's Wisdom

I say puke. If you hurl and she comes back, she's yours. If you blow chunks and she bolts, then it was never meant to be.
★ Mike Myers as Wayne Campbell in *Wayne's World*

I once thought I had mono for an entire year. It turned out I was just really bored.
★ Mike Myers as Wayne Campbell in *Wayne's World*

Chapter 5

I Yam What I Yam:
Coming of Age and
Coming-Out Movies

Who am I? What am I? Where did I develop this unusual taste for yams topped with miniature marshmallows? And why does everybody make such a fuss when I mix animal prints with purple patent leather?

The movies in this chapter feature quirky and unmanageable young heroines who aren't afraid to speak up and act out. By insisting on being themselves, they make the world a more colorful and interesting place, just because they're in it.

When you're learning how to live with the clashing hues and mixed prints and plaids of your unique personality, watch these Coming of Age and Coming-Out Movies, and celebrate your true colors.

■ *But I'm a Cheerleader* (1999)
Stars: Natasha Lyonne, Clea DuVall
Director: Jamie Babbit
Writers: Jamie Babbit, Brian Wayne Peterson

Megan (Natasha Lyonne) is a cheerleader living in a cozy suburban split-level, watching TV in a walnut-paneled family room, and eating meat-and-potato dinners (minus the meat). What could be more red-blooded and all-American than that? Trouble is, while Megan is French-kissing the captain of the football team (badly), she's thinking about the supple thighs and pert breasts of her spirit squad sisters instead of what's going on underneath Jared the jock's athletic cup.

In a bizarre twist, Megan's enriched white bread friends and family stage an intervention and out Megan. They tell Megan that her vegetarianism, the pictures of girls in sports bras in her locker, and her obvious lack of enthusiasm while kissing the captain of the football team are all dead giveaways that despite her pleated skirt and her perky pom-poms, Megan is a full-fledged sister of Sappho.

Now you know you've got some developmental stumbling blocks to hurdle when your parents out *you*, and things get even more difficult for Megan when they ship her off to a "Sexual Redirection Center" to "get her back on the straight and narrow." Fortunately, what awaits Megan at Mary Brown's Sexual Redirection Center is a vagina pink world, filled with lots of latex and a bevy of beautiful and sexually starved teenage lesbians, all engaged in a very unconvincing attempt to behave like straight girls. While practicing gender-appropriate behavior, like changing diapers and vacuuming, Megan meets the irreverent and darkly sensual Graham (Clea DuVall), and rather than learning the error of her ways, Megan winds up understanding the truth about herself.

This is a great movie to watch when you need a little team spirit to rally your flagging drive, and cheer you on through the goalposts of self-discovery, no matter what the color of your pom-poms.

■ *Love and Basketball* (2000)
Stars: Sanaa Lathan, Omar Epps, Alfre Woodard, Regina Hall
Director and Writer: Gina Prince-Bythewood

Monica Wright's (Sanaa Lathan) got game, but unfortunately, the world isn't exactly giving her a standing ovation. She has a jealous mom (Alfre Woodard) with a martyr complex, an unsupportive boyfriend (Omar Epps) who wants to outshine her on the court, a public that thinks her aggressiveness is terribly unattractive and unfeminine, and a sister (Regina Hall) who thinks all Monica's troubles could be erased if she would just do something with her hair already. Worse, in the pre–WNBA era, Monica's chosen career will require relocating overseas, where she has no support system. Will Monica find a way to shoot hoops without compromising her selfhood, disappointing her mother, and having to give up all hope for a romance with a man who can respect her love of the game? Or will she have to keep lying to herself about how basketball "just isn't any fun anymore"?

When the world is telling you that you can't, and your heart is telling you that you can, we bet this story about expectations and limitations, self-acceptance, and having to modify one's dreams will resonate for you. Besides, the honest and fresh depiction of the tense relationship between an ambitious young woman and a homemaker mom is, alone, something you've got to check out.

▪ *Sabrina* (1954)
Stars: Audrey Hepburn, Humphrey Bogart, William Holden
Director: Billy Wilder
Writers: Billy Wilder, Samuel A. Taylor, Ernest Lehman, based on the play
Sabrina Fair by Samuel A. Taylor

What's a girl to do when she becomes aware that she has not yet ripened into her most fabulous self? Well, we have to agree with Sabrina Fairchild (Audrey Hepburn): when in doubt, Paris is always a good idea. And so this ponytailed, jumper-clad, and freshly scrubbed young woman leaves behind her heartaches, gets the hell off of Long Island, and heads to cooking school in gay Paree, where she learns to break eggs one-handed under the watchful eye of a master chef, all the better to prepare her for . . .

Okay, we're not sure what the ability to whip up a perfect béarnaise sauce does for Sabrina, but hey, this new skill is the least of what this ex-wallflower brings home. Once merely the chauffeur's daughter, she is transformed by her experiences abroad into the height of Parisian sophistication, with a pixie cut, smart suit, matching luggage, and a French poodle to accessorize the new Sabrina. David Larrabee (William Holden), the wealthy playboy to whom she was invisible before, doesn't even recognize her and fawns over Sabrina, not guessing that she's been aching for him for years. But now that Sabrina has poise and confidence, she can take her pick of the litter, and David's brother, Linus (Humphrey Bogart), may be a more delectable treat, even if he is a little old to play her leading man.

If you know it's your time to blossom, but you can't afford the Air France fares, then break out a block of Brie and some crusty bread and get a lesson from Sabrina in the power of self-confidence.

◑ *So Nice They Made It Twice:* Avoid the woefully inferior remake with Julia Ormond, Greg Kinnear, and Harrison Ford, which doesn't have the magic of the original.

What I want to know is, who is this woman who's wearing my clothes, using my body?

★ Kristin Scott Thomas in *Random Hearts*

■ *Go Fish* (1994)
Stars: *Guinevere Turner, V. S. Brodie, Anastasia Sharp, T. Wendy McMillan, Migdalia Melendez*
Director: *Rose Troche*
Writers: *Rose Troche, Guinevere Turner*

This coming-out movie plays a lot like a lesbian *Real World*, featuring a carefully assembled urban family of young women who all seem to live in the same apartment, engaging in various personal intrigues and helping each other to cope and to grow by maintaining a steadfast connection to each other. And most everybody is pierced and/or tattooed and wears baggy pants. African American earth mother/professor Kia (T. Wendy McMillan) and her girlfriend, Evy (Migdalia Melendez), a spicy Latina divorcée with a Julia Roberts smile who isn't out to her family, try to set up their roommate, Max (Guinevere Turner), an Ivory girl who looks really cute in a baseball cap, with the bookish and bespectacled wallflower Ely (V. S. Brodie), who is enmeshed in a codependent long-distance nonrelationship. Got all that? Well, wait, there's more. Evy is outed to her mom and thrown out of the house, Kia takes her in, Ely gets a really outrageous haircut—and we mean really outrageous—and learns that if you can't be with the one you love, honey, love the one you're with. Oh, and Max continues to look really, really adorable in a baseball cap.

While it is refreshing to see a slice-of-life movie about real lesbians being real lesbians, we wished that a little more would have been discussed in this movie beyond the political value of presenting an up-close and personal look at lesbian life and fashion. But regardless of our frustration with the ideological vicissitudes of Ely's haircut, or the debates over the pros and cons of *honey pot* versus *beaver* as a euphemism for women's genitals, we do think that this movie is a reassuring reminder that you're never really alone as long as you express the love in your heart.

Freudian Slipups

Girl, Interrupted (1999)
Stars: Winona Ryder, Angelina Jolie, Whoopi Goldberg
Director: James Mangold
Writers: James Mangold, Lisa Loomer, Anna Hamilton
    Phelan, based on the memoir by Susanna Kaysen

Girl, Interrupted is yet another contribution to the adolescence-as-psychosis genre that reminds us all that for a sensitive teenager in a world of unsympathetic adults, insanity can be the only sane decision—although it's probably not a good idea to chase a bottle of aspirin with a quart of vodka, regardless of the severity of your maturational migraine.

And this movie will give you a migraine, once Lisa (Angelina Jolie), the relentless and extremely noisy metaphor for teen angst, shows up and inspires us all to start praying for the peace and quiet of the grave. This movie tries to send a positive message about the brave beauty of adolescent girls as they struggle to survive in a world that wants to stamp out teen spirit. Unfortunately, it makes a U-turn somewhere and heads back full speed for an early sixties morality that confuses growing pains with sociopathy.

Mid-howl, Lisa, who is supposed to be emblematic of the truth-telling bad

. . . continued

girl inside us all, becomes a sad and empty parasite who whines a lot. And our heroine Susanna (Winona Ryder), who just a few short months ago was a full-fledged Sylvia Plath–reading, upper-middle-class-value–questioning, filterless-cigarette–smoking teenage goddess of despair, becomes a boring girl next door who has learned how to just say no. Susanna says no to her best friend Lisa, no to her dark side, and no to a somewhat promising coming-of-age film that ultimately chickens out and stops short of saying something really useful about rebellious teenagedom like hey world, chill out, can't you see we're only dancing?

■ *Mask* (1985)
Stars: Cher, Eric Stoltz, Sam Elliott, Laura Dern
Director: Peter Bogdanovich
Writer: Anna Hamilton Phelan, based on the true story of Rocky Dennis

Rusty (Cher), a big-haired rock-and-roll mama, loves leather miniskirts and all things biker—the machines, the men, the jackets, and the four-letter words. Her son, Rocky (Eric Stoltz), is a scrawny teen with long, frizzy red hair, a kid who loves the 1952 Brooklyn Dodgers and dreams of motorcycling across Europe. He simply refuses to get depressed despite having an extremely disfiguring and terminal disease that causes his skull to grow huge and distorted, giving him a leonine appearance.

In many ways, Rocky is the typical teen, insecure about being accepted and convinced at times that he's a "freak," but his atypical mother has managed to instill in him a powerful sense of self-confidence that she herself lacks. So while Rocky has a remarkably mature approach to life, it's Rusty who is holding on to the trappings of adolescent rebellion, and acting out in a destructive way. Can Rocky's maturity inspire Rusty to set aside her notions about how it's no fun to be a grown-up and make her take up the mantle of being a responsible parent?

This is a great movie to watch if you're still struggling with accepting yourself. The courageous Rocky shows us that true maturity means making peace with ourselves and being the agents of our own lives regardless of our circumstances.

Freudian Slipups

Coyote Ugly (2000)
Stars: John Goodman, Piper Perabo, Adam Garcia,
*   Tyra Banks*
Director: David McNally II
Writer: Gina Wendkos

Dancing on a bar top in a belly shirt in a New York City meat-packing district watering hole was never really our idea of a positive rite of passage. But in the world of *Coyote Ugly*, where the booze is one hundred proof and water is illegal, the bar rail is what separates the girls from the coyotes. Violet (Piper Perabo), a naive Jersey girl who has taken good care of her daddy (John Goodman) ever since her mom died, moves to the Big Apple to pursue her dreams of being a songwriter. But she's never going to make the grade until she can do the one thing that her mom could never do—overcome her stage fright and sing her song to the world. Aided by her boyfriend, Kevin O'Donnell (Adam Garcia), Violet finds the courage to climb up on the bar top of life, rip off her clothes, and sing along with the jukebox really appealingly. Crowd goes wild. Record company execs line up to sign her. Boyfriend proposes.

Yeah, right.

For one thing, the last time we checked out the watering holes in the meat-packing district, we saw a lot of things on the bar tops, but no flaxen-haired maidens dancing and singing their way to the Rock Star Hall of Fame. Although we think we did see a platinum blonde at one joint licking the bar rail. And when we took our first steps toward gaining the courage and the confidence to pursue our dreams, it took a lot more than a flat tummy and the ability to dance tantalizingly in front of a barroom full of horny guys. Frankly, those tricks are for kids.

▪ *The Sandy Bottom Orchestra* (2000)

Stars: Glenne Headley, Tom Irwin, Madeline Zima, Jane Powell
Director: Bradley Wigor
Writer: Joseph Maurer, based on the novel by Garrison Keillor and Jenny Lind Nilsson

Mythical small-town Sandy Bottom, Wisconsin, could benefit from a radical element—not necessarily a nose-ring–wearing anarchist, but a woman who can bring it a little high culture. Maybe it will be lifted out of its homogenized complacency by rabble-rouser Ingrid Green (Glenne Headley), a former concert pianist who settled in Sandy Bottom when she married a dairy farmer (Tom Irwin). Ingrid deeply loves her family and community, but she's a petition-circulating, letter-to-the-editor–writing Lutheran choir director who urges people to expand their limited repertoires. Ingrid is convinced that her well-meaning protests are about as welcome in ever-sunny Sandy Bottom as a discouraging word. Truly, she wants only to feel that she fits in, that her gifts are valued, and that she's doing something important.

With the local Dairy Days celebration looming, husband Norman gets a brilliant idea to raise up his fellow Sandy Bottomers and give Ingrid a prime opportunity to face the music once and for all—to admit she does want acceptance as much as she wants to be herself. Can Ingrid make her own kind of music and live in harmony with her neighbors too? Or will she have to tone down in order to fit in?

Watch *Sandy Bottom Orchestra* when you feel intimidated by the thought of singing your own song from the heart, and you'll be reassured that all God's children have a place in the choir.

Ugh! This town! Nothing but teeny little minds and great big lawn-mowers!

★ Glenne Headley as Ingrid in *Sandy Bottom Orchestra*

Nancy's Momentous Minutiae: Lingerie Legends

Once, in the 1930s, someone in the costume department at RKO swiped Katharine Hepburn's signature pants from her dressing room. Rather than don a dress (as the Hollywood moguls always wanted her to do), Hepburn insisted on walking around in her underwear until the missing slacks were returned.

William Randolph Hearst, incensed by Jean Harlow's appearance at one of his dinner parties in a filmy white evening gown sans underwear, had someone tell Miss Harlow that she had better change. Harlow returned to the party in a coat, still wearing the offending gown underneath—and no lingerie.

▪ *Desert Hearts* (1986)
Stars: Helen Shaver, Patricia Charbonneau, Audra Lindley
Director: Donna Deitch
Writers: Jane Rule, Natalie Cooper

Okay, how can you argue with a lesbian movie that includes a ranch house in the desert full of divorcées, a coltish and free-spirited ranch hand who frequently wears cowboy boots, and a blond, Catherine Deneuvian enigma who drifts into town in search of a new sexual identity? Getting the idea? This movie is like a lesbian's *Lady Chatterley's Lover*. Vivian Bell (Helen Shaver), an elegant and extremely repressed literature professor from New York City, takes a room in a ranch in the desert outside Reno, where women live awaiting their quickie divorces. Vivian, who stands in that purgatory between her old life and the unknown future, finds herself strangely drawn to Cay (Patricia Charbonneau), the lithesome and uninhibited stepdaughter of the ranch's Ruth-like owner (Audra Lindley). What ensues is an all-consuming and passionate romance that gives new birth to both women, and includes some very steamy love scenes shot in real time. Watch this movie when you need a reminder that whether a romance continues or comes to an end, the exchange of true love transforms our lives forever for the better.

Reel to Real

Desert Hearts was the first lesbian-themed movie written and directed by women. It is also the first lesbian love story that allowed its lovers to have a happy ending.

▪ *Pinky* (1949)
Stars: Jeanne Crain, Ethel Waters, William Lundigan, Ethel Barrymore
Director: Elia Kazan
Writers: Philip Dunne, Dudley Nichols, based on the novel by Cid Ricketts Sumner

Up in Boston, no one asks Nurse Patricia "Pinky" Johnson (Jeanne Crain) a lot of questions, and she's not about to offer information. Fact is, Pinky may look white, but she was raised by her grandmother, a black laundress (Ethel Waters) living in a swamp down south, which in the pre–Civil Rights Act era meant Pinky was considered "colored"—not exactly the kind of pedigree those Boston blue bloods like to record in their social register.

As the movie opens, Pinky's starting to realize that her decision to pass as white up north may have its advantages—like, say, being treated as a human being—but the cost of denying a part of herself may be higher than she'd thought. She is pressured by her white fiancé, Dr. Thomas Adams (William Lundigan), to keep mum about herself—really, he's not prejudiced, it's just, well, there's no real need to mention certain things . . . *uh-huh*. But if Pinky, who has returned south to work out some unfinished business, stays in the neighborhood, it means she'll have to put up with the cruel treatment dished out by the local whites. Given her options, is it any wonder Pinky's lovely face has a perpetual look of contempt and disgust?

Frankly, we have a hard time understanding how young women like Pinky survive without a nice quiet place in which to scream their lungs out, or at least a Walkman and a

Queen Latifah CD to listen to while kick boxing. But then, for all her confusion, Pinky's got one unshakable sense of entitlement that will, in the end, make her stronger than her most powerful adversary and lead her to make the choices that are right for her.

If you've been feeling pressured to compromise and deny who you are in order to fit in, check out *Pinky* for a lesson in the power of self-acceptance.

Hoopskirt Dreams

When you're tired of rummaging through all the hideous shirtdresses and retro-seventies peasant blouses on the racks at the mall, pop in one of these Hoopskirt Dreams flicks and escape to a world where silk, satin, and glorious color envelop women with non–Barbie doll bodies.

Thrill of a Romance (1945)

Poor Esther Williams has been dumped by her new husband, but with all these beautiful costumes to distract her, how can she help but have a fabulous time in Beverly Hills? First, she's got trunks full of lovely dresses, including a bridal outfit featuring—what else, considering her natatorial nature?—a mermaid gown. She also shows up in several discreet yet sexy one-piece bathing suits, some with matching tiaras (we're big on tiaras for afternoons poolside, aren't you?). Even the supporting characters show up in amazing outfits, like the gal who dons a black off-the-shoulder sheath with a long black chiffon scarf draped around her neck and shoulders, accented, of course, with a long cigarette holder. So very vintage Barbie Solo-in-the-Spotlight. Why, with outfits like these, getting dumped doesn't seem so bad after all! *Costumes by Irene.*

. . . continued

Forever Amber (1947)

We hate to see a spirited gal like Amber St. Clair chastened by a moralistic ending imposed upon her by the Production Code, but this movie's worth watching for the elegant costumes alone. Amber, a former Puritan turned Elizabethan lady of the court, is about the best-dressed social climber we've ever come across on film. After ditching the prim gray dresses and bonnets, she decks herself out in ostrich hats the size of the entire bird, cornflower-blue and pink-and-gray silk dresses with intricately detailed princess bodices, and a form-fitting lime sheath with a blue satin cape that's utterly sumptuous. Honey, why chase after a foppish and hypocritical boyfriend when you can spend your time shopping for clothes like these? *Costumes by René Hubert.*

Madame X (1966)

Former San Francisco shop girl Lana Turner marries up and gains herself a wardrobe budget worthy of, well, a movie star. Her everyday monochromatic dresses don't much excite us, but we'll take the mint-green chiffon evening gown and that black dress with the plunging neckline punctuated by the fatal turquoise scarf. And could we please have just *one* of those amazing drop diamond earring sets she has for every outfit? *Costumes by Jean Louis, jewelry by David Webb, furs by Ben Kahn.*

Titanic (1997)

We can't decide what delights us most in this movie: the pea-green silk gown with the fiery sash and droopy lace cuffs? The navy-pinstripe-on-cream traveling suit? The ruby-colored, empire waist evening frock with black lace overdress? The royal-blue velvet and silk number with gossamer shawl? Or the fact that Kate Winslet wasn't bullied into starving away all those healthy curves to fit into these confections? High-five us on the size twelve, sister! But what a shame that all those gowns have to sink to the bottom of the deep

. . . continued

blue sea. Really, conspicuous consumption as a metaphor for the arrogance of man in the rational age never looked so yummy. *Costumes by Deborah L. Scott.*

Elizabeth (1998)

If you're stuck living in a drafty and damp castle, dodging would-be assassins and dealing with major office politics, you might as well have a wardrobe of dresses made of layer upon layer of emerald velvet and rich embroidered silk in shades of gold and scarlet, a closet full of crowns, and one of those white fur capes with the black spots that probably do wonders for keeping a girl warm when the cold winds of political sabotage are blowing. And that humongous carnival night headdress with the autumnal theme—no wonder Elizabeth has to recline in a gondola when she wears it! But we think we'll forgo the shaved forehead, the white lead makeup, and the poisoned dress that kills the handmaid (that'll teach her to borrow clothes without asking permission!). *Costumes by Alexandra Byrne.*

Stupid Guy Quotes

What Stanley needs is a firm hand—somebody with gumption enough to make her toe the line, a man with enough red blood in him to boss her.

★ Charles Coburn as Uncle William in *In This Our Life*

We had fun. I took you to the dump. We shot some rats.

★ Sean Penn as Emmet Ray in *Sweet and Lowdown*

Nobody's looking for a puppeteer in today's wintry economic climate.

★ John Cusack as Craig Schwartz in *Being John Malkovich*

Freudian Slipups

All I Wanna Do (1998) *(also known as* **Strike!***)*
Stars: *Kirsten Dunst, Gaby Hoffman, Heather Matarazzo,*
    Lynn Redgrave, Tom Guiry
Director and Writer: *Sarah Kernochan*

Oh, how we wanted to love this movie. It's got a girl-power message about the value of single-sex schools for young women. It's got a smart but sullen girl (Gaby Hoffman) who gets over just wanting to lose her virginity and discovers through her friendships with other young women that there are bigger dreams to dream. It's got scathing lines about the shockingly limited choices that smart young women faced in 1963. So what's not to like?

For one thing, why are we supposed to cheer on the male vigilantism of the gang of misfit boys when they help the girls out by beating up the nasty prepsters? Couldn't the girls solve the problem themselves, nonviolently? Also, we hated how the Kirsten Dunst character—who fights the hardest to keep the school from merging with the all-boy academy down the road—gets one kiss from a drunken prepster (Tom Guiry) and then is all for coed education. And do we have to see gratuitous shots of teenage girls in lingerie and a mass puking scene? Yep, once you let the boys in the clubhouse, things rapidly deteriorate into *Animal House* antics.

We wish the movie had simply stuck with the original premise that all-girl institutions are valuable because their young female students are able to pursue their educations without wasting energy worrying about whether the boys will reject them for being too smart and not pretty enough. So we say save the rental money and honor your younger sisters by sending a check off to your own boarding school or buying a few boxes of Girl Scout cookies instead.

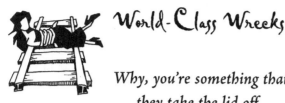

World-Class Wrecks

Why, you're something that flies out of a jar when they take the lid off.

★ Joan Crawford as Sally Parker to Clark Gable as Michael Anthony in *Love on the Run*

Ms. Perky (Allison Janney): People perceive you as somewhat . . .
Katarina Stratford (Julia Stiles): Tempestuous?
Ms. Perky: "Heinous bitch" is the term used most often.

★ from *10 Things I Hate About You*

■ Theodora Goes Wild (1936)

Stars: Irene Dunne, Melvyn Douglas
Director: Richard Boleslawski
Writer: Sidney Buchman, based on a story by Mary McCarthy

Lynnfield, Connecticut, population 4,426, prides itself on its civic responsibility, clean streets, and high moral standards, which are upheld by several dozen crotchety old broads in shapeless polka-dot dresses and fussy little hats. These ladies of the literary circle flare their nostrils and harumph over a new, steamy, Peyton Place–esque best seller. Calmly affirming the ladies' indignation is the dimpled and well-coiffed Theodora, a young woman who wouldn't dream of reading such trash. No, she just writes it.

Yes, Theodora Lynn (Irene Dunne) has a secret life as Caroline Adams, hotshot author. When she sneaks into New York City for a quick meeting with her editor, she captures the attention of book jacket artist Michael (Melvyn Douglas), who follows her to Lynnfield, determined to let the spirited Caroline out of her cage. And so Theodora goes wild, celebrating her selfhood and condemning the stifling atmosphere of small-town life, only to discover that her new beau has a cage of his own that needs rattling. Of course, she returns the favor.

If you're itching for a chance to stand up and spout off, we bet this story about a truth speaker who wakes up a sleepy town and finds true love along the way will leave you ready to launch your own little revolution.

> ⚠ Warning Label: *When you pop this one in, you'll have to time-warp back to a far more innocent era to see the humor value in the scene where Henry corners Theodora in her apartment in a courtship gesture that borders on date rape.*

Stupid Guy Quotes

It's important to think. It's what separates us from lentils.

★ Jeff Bridges as Jack Lucas in *The Fisher King*

I don't want to pump any sunshine up your skirt, but you have a future at Food World.

★ William Daniels as Mr. Summers in *Oh, God!*

■ *Trekkies* (1997)
Stars: Denise Crosby, Brent Spiner
Director: Roger Nygard

We all have our secret indulgences that we're embarrassed to admit to, but rather than risk being ridiculed, most of us stash the old REO Speedwagon albums in the closet or hide our cheesy romance novel collection in the darkness under the bed. But then there are those brave souls who confidently and openly proclaim their passion, unafraid of what anyone else will say about the rubber prosthesis glued on their forehead to emulate a Klingon, or their nerdy polyester, quasi-militaristic, unisex jumpsuit complete with plastic communicator pin.

Alright, so maybe they aren't so much brave as they are completely deluded about the reasons behind their need to immerse themselves in an alternate identity, a fictional universe, and a fantasy sex life. In fact, in this documentary about Trekkies (or Trekkers—apparently even their name is a subject of great philosophical debate among them), there's an awful lot of sexual sublimation going on: adult women lovingly cataloging hundreds of virtually identical photos of actor Brent Spiner; men sending actress Denise Crosby X-rated sketches of her; an entire subculture of pornographic novellas featuring Kirk and Spock, and a lot of fellas who are just a little bit too fascinated by the operation of the *Enterprise*'s thrusters. Hey, we're all for the higher ideals espoused in the Gene Roddenberry vision of the future, but we also feel that there comes a point when one should, well, get laid.

But then, despite all the surrealism in the world of Trekkies—the dentist who decorates his office like a starship and the female juror who attended the Whitewater trial in her Federation uniform—there really is something to their shared vision. Imagine a society devoid of greed, materialism, selfishness, and bigotry; a *Star Trek* reality in which the uniqueness of each individual is valued.

Watch this movie when you want reassurance that even when you're at your quirkiest you deserve to be treated with dignity and respect. Then proudly don your uniform of choice and go forth boldly.

Freudian Slipups

10 Things I Hate About You (1999)
Stars: *Julia Stiles, Heath Ledger, Andrew Keegan,*
  Joseph Gordon-Levitt, Larisa Oleynik
Director: *Gil Junger*
Writers: *Karen McCullah Lutz, Kirsten Smith*

After the success of *Clueless,* a clever update of Jane Austen's *Emma* set among the Valley Girl set, someone came up with the bright idea to transfer the plot of Shakespeare's *Taming of the Shrew* to Southern California. Unfortunately, the message here is deeply offensive—that all a teenage girl needs to get comfortable with the thought of "doing the deed" is the right guy. And this from female screenwriters!

Just as in the original play, a father tells his youngest daughter, Bianca (Larisa Oleynik), that she can't hook up with her boyfriend (Andrew Keegan) until her shrill-tongued older sister, Kat (Julia Stiles), can find a mate. Now, in Shakespeare's day the father was motivated by the desire to marry off both his children so that they wouldn't be left without a source of income; in this version, he's just got a weird whim and deeply hypocritical ideas about sexuality. We think anyone who sends his daughters to school braless in spaghetti-strap tank tops and then makes them parade around the house in pregnancy prostheses has some major sexual issues of his own.

Kat turns out to be a shrew not because she fears losing a precious piece of herself when she marries (the bard's version), but because she's been sexually mistreated by a boy in the past—just bring her the right boy and she'll be cured of her frigidity that manifests as bitchiness. Oh, now there's a lovely message—bitchy and abused girls just need a good lay. Worse, how do we learn that Kat has finally gotten over her mistrust of young men and is no

. . . *continued*

longer "uptight"? She helps her new boyfriend sneak out of class by distracting the male teacher by flashing him. How liberating.

Much as we adored watching Heath Ledger go from cocky bad boy to sensitive hunk in this one—yes, his sexy rendition of the corny "Can't Take My Eyes Off of You" did make us sigh in delight—we think we'll stick with Shakespeare's original.

Words to Live By

It is the worst kind of yellowness to be so scared of yourself that you put blindfolds on rather than deal with yourself. To face ourselves—that's the hard thing. The imagination—that's God's gift, to make the act of self-examination bearable.

★ Will Smith as Paul in *Six Degrees of Separation*

Chapter 6

"Oh, Her? She's My Sister.": Trust Issue Movies

"The check is in the mail." "The computer is down." "My wife doesn't understand me." If you're buried under an avalanche of life's little snow jobs and can't find a shovel, maybe it's time you start listening to that little voice inside that says, "My life is becoming a woman-in-jeopardy thriller. Perhaps I should lock up the silver, install an emergency generator, and work on my character judgment skills."

In these Trust Issue Movies, our heroines learn the hard way that trust has to be earned, and that we must listen to our instincts as well as our common sense instead of rushing to judgment. So if you've been repressing a few suspicions of late, or have been digging for the truth and coming up with nothing more than another layer of confusion, watch these movies and enjoy the twenty-twenty vision that comes from being an observer instead of a participant.

■ *Sudden Fear* (1952)

Stars: Joan Crawford, Jack Palance
Director: David Miller
Writers: Lenore Coffee, Robert Smith, based on Edna Sherry's novel Sudden Fear

San Francisco heiress and playwright Myra Hudson (Joan Crawford) doesn't have anything against actor Lester Blaine (Jack Palance), it's just that he doesn't seem like leading-man material. So she has him fired, blowing his big break and probably destroying his career. Then, what a coincidence! Lester shows up on the very same cross-country train, shrugging off the fact that Myra has destroyed his chance at stardom and quoting her delightfully romantic dialogue back to her. How sweet of him to remember her carefully penned words! And how awful that once they've become husband and wife, he feels intimidated by her money and position. Really, he must set up some bank accounts for himself and not say another word about it.

Yup, Myra's just a little bit too trusting of a man so quick to forgive her that you'd think she had merely misspelled his hometown in *Playbill*. And when Lester moves into her life, she'd better start paying closer attention to his subtle cues that something sinister is going to happen in the third act. *Mental Note:* Heiresses who think they have no enemies ought to keep lots of dictating machines and hidden microphones throughout their homes.

Watch this one when you've been a little too quick to trust someone and be glad that at least you don't have to plot your own personal film noir adrenaline-run escape from the consequences of your actions.

 ## Stupid Guy Quotes

You are all the women in my life—you are the sister I never had, the mother I've almost forgotten. . . . There isn't a relationship you can name which exists between a man and a woman in which I wouldn't say "let it be you."

★ Jack Palance as Lester Blaine in *Sudden Fear*

▪ *The Astronaut's Wife* (1999)
Stars: Johnny Depp, Charlize Theron
Director and Writer: Rand Ravich

This is the ultimate "this is not the man I married" movie about a woman who must learn that even something that looks like a duck and quacks like a duck may not actually be a duck at all.

Astronaut Spencer Armacoust (Johnny Depp) and his comrade Alex Streck (Nick Cassavetes) are lost to ground control for two minutes after experiencing an explosion while on a space walk to repair a wounded satellite. When Spencer returns to earth, his girlfriend Jillian (Charlize Theron) finds that he just isn't himself—he starts pounding the black Jack until the wee hours of the morning and listening to radios that aren't turned on. And for some reason or another, the normally placid and gentle Spencer has become a real wild animal in the sack. Poor Jillian can't figure out whom she is getting into bed with every night.

The Astronaut's Wife is a story about what happens when the honeymoon is over and that kind considerate guy to whom you said "I do" turns into an unfriendly alien with big pointy teeth who wants to infiltrate your atmosphere and colonize your planet. This movie reminds us that when that little voice in your head is telling you that this isn't the man you married, it probably isn't.

Words to Live By

"Can't" lives on Won't Street.
★ Philip Seymour Hoffman as Rusty in *Flawless*

▪ *Six Degrees of Separation* (1993)
Stars: Stockard Channing, Will Smith, Donald Sutherland, Ian McKellen,
   Mary Beth Hurt, Bruce Davison
Director: Fred Schepisi
Writer: John Guare

This is the movie that popularized that idea about everybody on the earth only being separated by six degrees. Roughly translated, this means that if you want to meet Kevin Bacon it'll take six people to put you in touch. Or something like that. We never did quite get the mathematics of this movie. But basically, it's about a young man (Will Smith) who manages to con the New York social set with a good vocabulary, a celebrity pedigree, and a really good prep school blazer.

Six Degrees of Separation is a good reminder of how vulnerable we all are when we trust somebody based on snap judgments we make about the quality of his footwear, or how many Oscar nominations his father has received, and don't really see past the surface to the truth of our experience. At any given moment we are all only six degrees away from danger or redemption, so it pays to keep our eyes and our minds open.

Famous Last Words

Peggy, you know what a penis is? Stay away from it!

★ Barbara Harris as Peggy Sue's mom
in *Peggy Sue Got Married*

The Handy Hunk Chart Key

Hunk Ratings:

The Passionate Priests

WPBM = *Well-Placed Beauty Mark* **RUM** = *Raw Unpredictable Masculinity* **SPA** = *Six-Pack Abs* **RGH** = *Really Good Hair* **DD** = *Drowsy Drawl* **TIWL** = *That Irresistible Wounded Look* **APFM** = *A Poetic Flair for Metaphor* **DMCA** = *Devil-May-Care Attitude* **ASD** = *Aristocratic, Suave, and Debonair* **BE** = *Bedroom Eyes* **EGL** = *Exotic Good Looks* **EMT** = *Eyes Moist with Tears* **FSG** = *Feckless Schoolboy Grin* **PBE** = *Piercing Blue Eyes* **SIN** = *Smoldering, Inscrutable, and Noble* **TSHT** = *That Sexy Homicidal Thing* **CSD** = *Confidently Self-Deprecating*

The Handy Hunk Chart

Wes Bentley
WPBM, TIWL, SIN, APFM, EMT

Top Drool Pics: *American Beauty, The Claim, Soul Survivors*

There's nothing like a priest of love with dark, piercing eyes and a ski cap whose heart bleeds for the beauty of all creation to get our hearts pumping. Add a poetic flair for metaphor, a courageous heart, a fragile soul, and the most amazing facial peaks and valleys this side of the Continental Divide, shake vigorously, and you've got Wes Bentley, who makes us all just want to kiss it and make it better. Especially if we can kiss it right in that subtle hollow just beneath his left ear, where the resolute jawline meets the fertile delta of his mastic muscle. ▪

Gabriel Byrne
RGH, SIN, TSHT, BE

Top Drool Pics: *Stigmata, The Man in the Iron Mask, Miller's Crossing, End of Days, Little Women, Polish Wedding, Point of No Return*

It's true, we ached for Gabriel Byrne when he played a gentlemanly, poor yet honest scholar, a beleaguered yet loyal musketeer, and a priest ready to sacrifice his life for an innocent girl. How cruel the world is, refusing to conform to his sense of honor! But for all his smoldering passion for truth and justice, somehow, when Byrne takes a turn toward the nasty, he gets us all the more hot and bothered. Hey, it's not every man who can make a paternalistic trainer of international assassins sexy. And as Satan? Well, let's face it, he is hot hot hot. ▪

■ *Invasion of the Body Snatchers* (1978)

Stars: Donald Sutherland, Brooke Adams, Leonard Nimoy,
    Jeff Goldblum
Director: Philip Kaufman
Writer: W. D. Richter, based on the novel The Body Snatchers
    by Jack Finney

So he got up off the couch and emptied the garbage of his own accord, then gave away his tickets to the ball game, and now is mumbling something about attending a meeting at work instead? Yeah, you know what's up. He's been taken over by aliens and is plotting the end of human civilization as we know it.

Alright, maybe you are jumping to conclusions, but *Invasion of the Body Snatchers* is a chilling reminder of the importance of staying awake and recognizing when something new is in the wind.

In this case, what's blowing into town is spores from outer space that grow into pod people devoid of soul and emotion. As health inspector Matthew Bennell (Donald Sutherland) and his assistant Elizabeth (Brooke Adams) try to convince someone, any-one, that something very sinister is happening, they run up against major denial and de-mands for more and more evidence. Their arrogant psychiatrist friend Dr. David Kibner (Leonard Nimoy) insists that they are being illogical (yeah, sure, that's what he said to Bones about those aliens). Not being *Star Trek* fans, Elizabeth and Matthew listen to Kibner and lose a lot of valuable time. Frankly, they just don't know where to turn, but they do figure out pretty quickly that the reality of the forces that destroy our souls and turn us into pod people is that "they get you when you're asleep." Isn't that always the case?

Invasion of the Body Snatchers isn't just a terrific horror flick that'll get your blood pump-ing, it's a cautionary tale about the importance of staying vigilant, listening to your own in-stincts, and playing it cautious with others instead of instantly revealing what you know to whomever you meet. Believe us, the last visual of Donald Sutherland before the credits roll will stick in your head as a reminder of those particular truths.

Women We Wish We Could Go for a Beer With

Barbara Stanwyck—On-screen (especially pre–Production Code) she was smart, funny, loyal, and could talk her way out of just about any sort of trouble, which are all traits we like in a drinking buddy.

Christina Ricci—We'd like to hit one of those poorly illuminated biker bars in the meat-packing district with Christina Ricci. And if anyone gets out of line, we'll let *her* tell the huge bearded guy with the tattoo that says "Love Hurts" to act Christlike.

Jean Harlow—Legend has it that despite her on-screen image as the brassy broad with the heart of gold, she was as sweet-natured, genuine, and fun as could be. But should she suggest we toast to King Puff Puff Puff, we'll just let her drink some Wallace Beery type under the table instead of us.

Susan Sarandon—We'd like to sit down with Susan Sarandon and have the usual, because whatever that woman is drinking, we want a gallon.

Parker Posey—We'd like to stop by the Dairy Queen with Parker Posey and reinvent the Blizzard.

Bette Davis—We love a self-made woman who unapologetically serves Chinese takeout to her guests and claims she slaved in the kitchen for hours, although if we went out on the town with Bette we'd choose an outdoor bar, given the amount of secondhand smoke she generates.

Salma Hayek—We have to toast anyone who can make the book business seem hot, sexy, and dangerous.

■ *East Side, West Side* (1949)
Stars: Barbara Stanwyck, James Mason, Ava Gardner
Director: Mervyn LeRoy
Writer: Isobel Lennart, based on the novel by Marcia Davenport

When Jessie Bourne (Barbara Stanwyck) discovers that Isabel Larson, the former paramour of her husband, Brandon (James Mason), is back in town, she smiles bravely and tells her friend that her plan is to do all the things she would do if she weren't afraid. So what does a classy gal with a home on New York City's Gramercy Park and flawless elocution have to fear from Isabel, a shameless hussy with a bullet bra (Ava Gardner, being as bad as bad can be)? Plenty, apparently, since good old Bran has a weakness for women, one he might have better luck overcoming if he'd come straight home as promised instead of lingering at the bar where he used to hang out with Isabel. A few scotch and waters later, you can pretty much guess there's gonna be some tabloidesque activity.

Luckily, Jessie is blessed with a deeply supportive mother (when she reveals the extent of her loyalty, you'll want to pound your fist in the air and shout, "Yeah!"), friends who truly care about the fragile state of her heart, and a would-be suitor who wants her to take her time coming to a resolution about her life. Hell, even strangers are looking out for Jessie's emotional well-being. No wonder she finds the strength to make the decision that's right for her, all while holding her head high and looking absolutely fabulous.

Vacillating about whether to work it out with your own philanderer? Jessie will inspire you to do the right thing, whatever it may be.

Stupid Girl Quotes

You have to understand Bran. Something in him hates the idea of being tied down, settled, responsible, but he'll change. You'll see. He'll change.

★ Jessie Bourne (Barbara Stanwyck) as the loyal wife in *East Side, West Side*

Stupid Guy Quotes

Just because a man has one perfect rose in his garden at home, it doesn't mean that he can't appreciate the flowers of the field.

★ James Mason as philanderer Brandon Bourne in *East Side, West Side*

Freudian Slipups

Casablanca (1942)
Stars: *Humphrey Bogart, Ingrid Bergman, Paul Henreid*
Director: *Michael Curtiz*
Writer: *Joan Alison, based on the play* Everybody Comes to
    Rick's *by Murray Burnett*

"You do the thinking for both of us," says Ilsa (Ingrid Bergman) to Rick (Humphrey Bogart), and there's a part of us that wants to yell, "Take control of your own destiny, sister! Don't you watch *Oprah?*!" But of course, one of the reasons we gals think this is one of the greatest love stories ever to grace the silver screen is that it feeds into our deeply dysfunctional need to surrender control to a man in order to abdicate responsibility for our lives. Here, of course, when an angry ex-lover is entrusted with a woman's fragile heart, he rises to the occasion: Rick saves Ilsa's life, makes her most difficult choice for her, sends her off with her husband, Victor Laszlo (Paul Henreid), and heals her of all the guilt that has been plaguing her since those lost halcyon days in Paris. Ilsa's got it made, because even if she finds herself unhappy being with Victor, she can blame someone else for her situation.

And while we're on the subject of Victor, can someone explain to us why he has to have an adoring and utterly selfless wife in order to carry on his noble work? Couldn't he spare just a *little* time and attention for Ilsa? Or at least recognize that she is sacrificing her happiness for his and do the noble thing: set her free? Maybe then Ilsa, fulfilled in her personal life, would have the courage, creativity, and drive to find her own way to serve the French Resistance—without giving up passion and romance.

Ah, but then we wouldn't have that airport scene and the reassurance that there are men out there who can be trusted to rescue us when we are betwixt and between. Until we women rewrite our internal scripts for romance, we guess Hollywood will just keep stoking the fire of our dysfunction.

▪ *Wife vs. Secretary* (1936)

Stars: Clark Gable, Myrna Loy, Jean Harlow, James Stewart

Director: Clarence Brown

Writers: Norma Krasna, John Lee Mahin, Alice Duer Miller, based on a Cosmopolitan *magazine article by Faith Baldwin*

Helen "Whitey" Wilson (Jean Harlow) can't help it if she's an uncommonly good-looking gal—she's just trying to do her job as an executive secretary and right arm to a high-powered publishing executive, Van Stanhope (Clark Gable). Okay, so Van lies to his wife, takes Whitey to Cuba, and goes drinking with her into the wee hours, forgetting to call the missus back home. Circumstantial evidence, all of it—at least this is what Linda Stanhope (Myrna Loy) tells herself at first. But then there are all those innuendoes from the people at the magazine, and even Van's own mom is convinced that he can't possibly be faithful to his wife when a platinum blonde in a tight skirt is his constant companion. And let's face it, ya got Gable, ya got Harlow, ya got the thirties studio system—there's got to be a hot kissing scene coming up, right?

Well, things aren't so predictable in this curious timepiece from an era when a gal was proud to have a glamour job that requires her to leave her fiancé—Dave (James Stewart)—at the theater and dash off to take dictation for the boss. Dave learns to respect women's career choices, Van learns the value of honesty in intimate relationships, Linda learns the importance of good communication skills, and we all learn that typecasting is ultimately unfair to everyone.

Watch this when you need a little reassurance that when you've invested in a sturdy boat, you won't be tipped by the first brisk breeze to hit your sails.

She's Got Humphrey Bogart Eyes

Nobody cut straight to the heart of the matter like Bogie's hard-boiled private dicks, who never took anything at face value and weren't afraid to ask the tough questions and get to the bottom of things. Through Bogart's eyes, we can see through every flimflam, recognize every

. . . continued

hidden agenda, and uncover the truth in the final sequence. Here are a couple of movies to help you develop a little of that Bogart twenty-twenty vision.

The Maltese Falcon (1941)
Stars: Humphrey Bogart, Mary Astor, Peter Lorre, Sydney Greenstreet
Director: John Huston
Writer: John Huston, based on the novel by Dashiell Hammett

When his partner is killed, Sam Spade (Humphrey Bogart) is determined to do something about it. He's drawn into a web of murderous intrigue surrounding the acquisition of an ancient falcon by a dame-in-distress (Mary Astor) who has lost track of the dividing line between truth and illusion. In order to solve his partner's murder and discover the whereabouts of the falcon, he must outrun the police, juggle three separate clients with opposing agendas, prevent his heart from overmastering his head and send the dame-in-distress up the river, as well as untangle enough plot strands to knit an afghan.

If you're feeling overwhelmed by the hidden agendas in your own whodunit, and your priceless treasure remains hidden from view, watch *The Maltese Falcon* and let Bogart remind you that not all that glitters is gold.

The Big Sleep (1946)
Stars: Humphrey Bogart, Lauren Bacall
Director: Howard Hawks
Writers: William Faulkner, Leigh Brackett, Jules Furthman, based on the
  novel by Raymond Chandler

Plotwise, nobody has really ever figured out what's going on in this movie, and that includes the film's director, most of the story's protagonists, and the author of the original novel. But that doesn't stop private eye Philip Marlowe

. . . continued

(Humphrey Bogart) from seeing straight through the underbelly to the heart of the matter. In the course of this classic noir crime thriller, Marlowe solves seven inexplicable and often implausible murders, many of which happen off-screen. He uncovers the mastermind behind a blackmail scheme, locates a missing soldier with the Irish Republican Army, engages in several double entendre–laden verbal volleys with the linguistically labile femme fatale Vivian (Lauren Bacall), and somehow always manages to wind up on top.

When your personal plotline has become incomprehensible, let Philip Marlowe show you that when there are "lots of guns around town and so few brains," it's best to call your own shots as long as you don't run afoul of the district attorney.

Noir Nuggets

I don't mind if you don't like my manners. I don't like them myself. They're pretty bad. I grieve over them on long winter evenings.
★ Humphrey Bogart as Philip Marlowe in *The Big Sleep*

The cheaper the crook, the gaudier the patter, eh?
★ Humphrey Bogart as Sam Spade in *The Maltese Falcon*

My guess might be excellent or it might be crummy, but Mrs. Spade didn't raise any children dippy enough to make guesses in front of a district attorney, and an assistant district attorney, and a stenographer.
★ Humphrey Bogart as Sam Spade in *The Maltese Falcon*

▪ *My Cousin Rachel* (1952)
Stars: Olivia de Havilland, Richard Burton
Director: Henry Koster
Writer: Nunnally Johnson, based on the novel by Daphne Du Maurier

We've all been there: blinded by love, dismissing as idle gossip all those stories about a certain person's tendencies toward lavish spending, ready to make excuses for overdrawn bank accounts and new clothes that look like they were designed by a Hollywood costumer (can we just say we looove those black sequined accents on Miss de Havilland's scrumptious gowns?). But if you think you're having a hard time getting to the truth behind those gentle, I-can-explain-everything-dear-including-the-poison-stashed-in-my-dresser-drawer smiles, this movie will reassure you that in love, it isn't always easy to figure out exactly what's what.

Oh, Philip (Richard Burton) is more than skeptical at first—he's absolutely positive that his late cousin Ambrose's widow, Rachel (Olivia de Havilland), had something to do with Ambrose's sudden and mysterious death. But that's before Rachel shows up at his estate, brown eyes warm with sympathy and sadness, her widow's weeds demurely encasing her lovely body. Rachel's been so looking forward to brewing for Philip that special "health" tea that Ambrose loved so (mental note: do an Internet search on those Italian herbs). A few fluttering eyelashes later, Philip's more than ready to take a sip from her cup, no matter how bitter the brew. But is Rachel quietly preparing an attack, or is she simply a loving but cautious woman out to secure her own interests?

Watch *My Cousin Rachel* when you need a break from overanalyzing your own suspicions, and remind yourself that you're not the only starry-eyed lover in the world who is taking a risk.

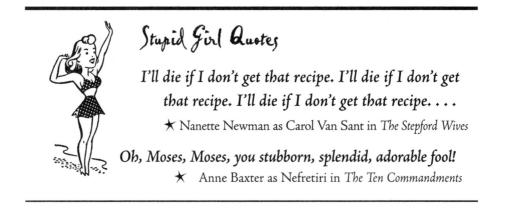

Stupid Girl Quotes

I'll die if I don't get that recipe. I'll die if I don't get that recipe. I'll die if I don't get that recipe. . . .
★ Nanette Newman as Carol Van Sant in *The Stepford Wives*

Oh, Moses, Moses, you stubborn, splendid, adorable fool!
★ Anne Baxter as Nefretiri in *The Ten Commandments*

▪ *Rosemary's Baby* (1968)
  Stars: *Mia Farrow, John Cassavetes, Ruth Gordon, Ralph Bellamy,*
    Charles Grodin, Sidney Blackmer
  Director: *Roman Polanski*
  Writer: *Roman Polanski, based on the novel by Ira Levin*

If the OB-GYN you were bullied into hiring tells you to trust him, saying, "Please don't read books . . . and don't listen to your friends either," it's probably time to start paying attention to your instincts and shopping for a second opinion. Perhaps, for example, wearing the good luck charm that belonged to the girl who jumped to her death the other night is not such a wise move. But it's 1965 and Rosemary Woodhouse (Mia Farrow) is a good girl in a yellow baby-doll dress and pigtails, so she trusts everyone but herself: doctors (Ralph Bellamy and Charles Grodin), her husband (John Cassavetes), and busybody neighbors (Ruth Gordon and Sidney Blackmer) who insist she use their doc, down their nasty herbal "vitamin" concoctions, and wear magic charms that stink of rotting fungus.

Rosemary represses her suspicions only to learn that all of her alleged allies are involved in an evil plot against her. Poor Rosemary just wanted a baby, a nice apartment, and one of those groovy new Vidal Sassoon low-maintenance cuts that are perfect for the independent modern gal on the go (no big surprise that her husband, Mr. "I'll make the decisions in this house," hates her new look). Unfortunately, she is so trusting that she overlooks mysterious accidents and sudden deaths happening all around her. It takes reading a book and talking with a couple of good friends to open her eyes to the lies that are making her life hell.

If the ending of this classic horror film doesn't convince you to start immediately demanding the truth from the people in your life, nothing will.

> ⚠ Warning Label: *If you know anything about goddess spir-*
> *ituality and modern paganism, the mythology in this film*
> *will make you wish that it were ethical to place evil*
> *curses on screenwriters.*

■ *East/West* (2000)

Stars: Sandrine Bonnaire, Oleg Menchikov, Sergueï Bodrov, Jr.,
Catherine Deneuve
Director: Régis Wargnier
Writers: Sergueï Bodrov, Jr., Roustam Ibraguimbekov, Louis Gardel,
Régis Wargnier

Feeling utterly baffled by the complexity and precariousness of your own entanglements? Here's a movie that'll convince you of the importance of taking a deep calming breath before jumping to any conclusions, particularly if you are living in a fascist regime.

So "All is forgiven and it is time to come home and rebuild"? Well, that's a lovely thought, but as soon as Alexei (Oleg Menchikov), a Russian expatriate, and his French wife, Marie (Sandrine Bonnaire), and son step off the boat and onto Russian soil that evening in 1946, they realize that taking the word of fascist dictators at face value is not such a wise idea. Within minutes shots ring out, a young man is dead, Marie's passport is in little pieces on the ground, and Alexei has to admit he has made a major mistake in judgment. Really, he'll get them out of Stalinist Russia just as soon as he can. If Marie could just be patient for a few decades.

Marie tries to lay low, but it's not exactly easy for this passionate Gaul who is miles from her homeland or even a French embassy. Soon her husband starts moving up the party ladder, and even has a brief affair with another woman who is more "understanding" of him, and Marie has to make some hard decisions about taking her fate into her own hands. Should she trust her husband, who shows no signs of planning an escape, or put her faith in a young man who has fallen hard for her and may be able to get her out of the country? Or is there another option, thanks to that French actress (Catherine Deneuve)?

Watch *East/West* when you know you need to take a little time out from the madness, and remember that choosing to do nothing is doing something. Hey, it'll all sort itself out eventually and in the meantime, at least you're not doing five years' hard labor in Siberia.

Chapter 7

Weeping, Wailing, and Gnashing of Teeth: Cathartic Weeper Movies

We know how it is—you've been a good girl and turned off all those inconvenient emotions that so unsettle everyone. You've bucked up, remained utterly professional and perfectly poised, and put on that great big Brownie smile. But now that you're home on your couch, just you and the cat, it's time to give yourself what you deserve—a good cry. Not a Hollywoodized cry, with gently fluttering eyelashes and a perfect glycerine tear trailing down your cheek. Oh, no—we mean a real sobfest, with sniffling and snorting and red eyes and honking into handfuls of premium facial tissues.

Deeply in need of an emotional catharsis followed by the inevitable uplift? Watch these Cathartic Weeper Movies and leave the stoic act behind.

▪ *Penny Serenade* (1941)
Stars: *Cary Grant, Irene Dunne*
Director: *George Stevens*
Writer: *Morrie Ryskind, based on a story by Martha Cheavens*

We know a woman who ruined a silk blouse crying over this film with its sentimental Victrola soundtrack; its message of how a woman can soften the hardest bachelor heart and woo him into love, marriage, and kids; and its darling Christmas pageant complete with precious little angels, warbly children's voices, and an astonishingly perfect "Silent Night" choir that brings us back to those hushed and magical Christmas Eves of the past. Then there's that break-your-heart scene in which Cary Grant grovels in front of a coldhearted judge, begging him to allow poor Cary to keep his adoptive daughter despite having lost his job due to the Depression. And how can you not choke up when childless Irene Dunne, trying so desperately to keep a stiff upper lip, enters the back bedroom of their new apartment only to be confronted with the cutest ducky and bunny wallpaper? It's all so unfair!

Yeah, the violins are a bit overwrought, and okay, we do get a little tired of filmmakers tugging at our heartstrings with a full-chorus rendition of "Auld Lang Syne" on yet another New Year's Eve to be remembered for always, but *Penny Serenade*'s story of loss, grief, and ultimate acceptance works for us again and again. Its portrayal of how pain can tear us apart, and how love and hope can bring us back together, is enough to make us feel that in the end, all will be right in our world, even if we don't have a crinkly-eyed Cary Grant grinning at us in oddly gratuitous close-ups.

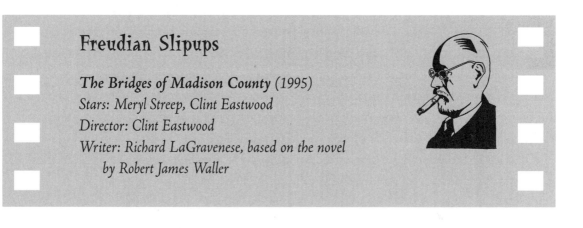

Freudian Slipups

The Bridges of Madison County (1995)
Stars: *Meryl Streep, Clint Eastwood*
Director: *Clint Eastwood*
Writer: *Richard LaGravenese, based on the novel
    by Robert James Waller*

The firmness of his starched cotton collar under your fingertips, the quiet strength of his forearms, the smell of his hair in the Iowa sunshine, the sight of his long graceful fingers curled around a handful of wildflowers he has picked just for you, and the feel of his arms around you as you slow-dance in the kitchen to a song on the radio. Yup, this was definitely worth missing the 1965 Iowa State Fair for. Hey, let the husband and kids admire the fifty species of rabbit—Robert Kincaid (Clint Eastwood) is in town, a roving hunk who fits perfectly into a pair of Levi's and doesn't even sweat on a hot summer day.

In this wonderfully erotic romance (based on an appallingly phallocentric and overwritten novel), Meryl Streep plays Francesca Johnson, an Italian war bride whose passionate nature has been long repressed. Francesca falls head-first into a four-day affair with Robert Kincaid, a *National Geographic* photographer. But despite the power of her desire for him and for a life that is more magical than the one she leads as a wife and mother in the middle of a corn-field somewhere, Francesca has been so tamed by the monotony and the re-strictiveness of rural America in the postwar years that when the time comes and Robert gives her that secret sign of his devotion and longing, she can only stare out into the cold blue rain and remain silent. All that is left is a fading memory and the promise that maybe, someday. . . . But then, framing the story, there's this whole B-plot involving her obnoxious kids whining about how now that Mom's dead they really don't want to know about the best four days of her life—and you know that the odds of Robert and Francesca having found a way to be together again are about as slim as finding an oasis of greenery among the endless maize.

It's hard not to weep bucketfuls when watching Francesca's sacrifices, espe-cially when you start getting in touch with your own feelings of being invali-dated. It's all so exquisitely painful. But if you think that repressing your own needs for a lifetime and living only for your family is noble, maybe it's time you take that crown of thorns off your head and demand a forum for your passion and encouragement for your dreams.

▪ *Untamed Heart* (1993)

Stars: Marisa Tomei, Christian Slater, Rosie Perez
Director: Tony Bill
Writer: Tom Sierchio

As anyone who's ever spent a winter in Minnesota can tell you, moments of sunlight breaking through the oppressive, steely-gray sky are rare, but if you are vigilant, an unexpected glint of radiance will catch your eye. For example, the busboy at the diner may well turn out to be a hauntingly beautiful Christian Slater type with a heart two sizes too big, a chivalrous streak as wide as the Great Plains, and a record collection of American jazz standards that makes for the perfect soundtrack to your star-crossed love affair with a beautiful boy-man.

Now, if painfully shy, vulnerable, and soft-spoken doesn't work for you, you probably will be a little creeped out by a guy who secretly follows you home and sneaks into your room to watch you sleep. But if you're fed up with having your heart broken by selfish Lotharios, you'll identify with the movie's heroine, Caroline (Marisa Tomei). How can you help but fall hard for a man who appears from nowhere to rescue you from a villainous cad and pound him into the ground, and yet can cry at your mere touch? Who can resist a leonine admirer with powerful biceps, who nevertheless sits quietly and watches his soft brown locks fall to the floor as you clip them, and who needs to be taken by the hand and led to your bed? A man who still believes in childhood fairy tales and becomes the prince of your dreams?

Then again, there's that nasty heart condition mucking everything up. Sure, it's the perfect metaphor for the fragility of life and love, but it also sets the stage for one of those heaving-sob endings. This movie will make you vow that, yes, you will love again, if only to enjoy the exquisite torment of crying your eyes out.

> ⚠ Warning Label: *Caroline's male-scripted reaction to a sexual assault will have you groaning, along with that line about him not having to love her back. Hey, just because we're in the mood for romantic tearjerkers doesn't mean we've turned into martyrs for love.*

Awww . . . this is one of those days that the pages of history teach us are best spent lying in bed.

★ Roland Young as Uncle Willie in *The Philadelphia Story*

■ *Bed of Roses* (1996)
Stars: Christian Slater, Mary Stuart Masterson, Pamela Segall
Director and Writer: Michael Goldenberg

Rootless Lisa Walker (Mary Stuart Masterson) believes that roses should have thorns and that nice guys who speak in soft and throaty voices and bow their heads ever so coyly as they smile up at you with soft brown eyes (Christian Slater in yet another sensitive-guy role) don't fall for women like her. Sure, she's a successful professional, and she has a deep and rewarding friendship with a female friend (Pamela Segall), but Lisa has a past so tragic, so lonely, so sorrow filled, that her entire life plays out to the tune of a moody Lilith Fair soundtrack and poignant slow-mo shots taken in the fading golden light of late afternoon.

After months of being involved with the narcissistic Danny (Josh Brolin) in a relationship of convenience, Lisa wants to believe in princes and magic kisses. Good thing she runs into the only man on the planet who has a habit of gazing into the windows of lonely women and yet isn't a stalker. What's more, he delivers flowers for a living and yet can afford an open and sunny Upper West Side studio that comes with full roof rights. And he not only calls but is ready to commit to marriage by the third date and sends a dozen roses every hour on the hour to convince her of his sincerity. Where's the catch?

The answer, of course, is that sometimes the most difficult part of making a relationship work is coming to believe in ourselves. Lisa must discover her sense of entitlement, put aside her fears, and dive into the unknown if she's to find happiness. And as we all know, accessing our deepest feelings of inadequacy always involves a good amount of throat-catching speeches, tearful confessions, and terrifyingly raw confrontations. Add in a little of Sarah MacLachlan's soft crooning and how can you help but let loose the waterworks?

Bev's Culinarytherapy: Food for Every Mood

Food for When You Could Weep a River

Okay, so these recipes are a little high in sodium content, but you're going to need something to replace all that salt you're depleting. So when you're feeling weepy, whip up one of these water-retention favorites, and then sit back and watch your feet swell.

The Braunschweiger Party Log

This is a recipe from Anita Crooks of the Catholic Church of the Resurrection in Smithtown, New York.

½ *pound bacon (full sodium)*	*8 ounces whipped cream cheese*
8 ounces braunschweiger (salted)	*1 box of your favorite high-salt crackers*

Fry bacon until crisp, and crumble. Take braunschweiger out of the plastic, making sure that you retain the log shape of the meat. Frost the log with whipped cream cheese, roll in bacon, chill, and serve with salty crackers.

Salt-and-Vinegar Potato Chips

Open a large bag of salt-and-vinegar potato chips. Serve promptly. And don't cry into the bag. It'll make the chips soggy.

Bacon Bloaters

This is a recipe from our friend John, who is one of the few men in existence who really understand a lot about retaining water. He whips

. . . continued

up a batch of these appetizers at every office Christmas party, and then stands back and watches the bosses bloat.

1 pound bacon   ½ pound dates

Roll each date into one strip of bacon and broil. When the bacon is almost crispy, stick a toothpick in them—they're done!

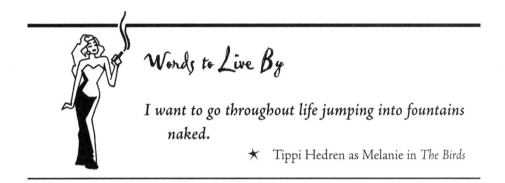

Words to Live By

I want to go throughout life jumping into fountains naked.

★ Tippi Hedren as Melanie in *The Birds*

▪ To Each His Own (1946)

Stars: Olivia de Havilland, John Lund, Mary Anderson, Phillip Terry
Director: Mitchell Leisen
Writers: Charles Brackett, Jacques Théry, based on a story by Charles Brackett

In this wonderful tearjerker, Olivia de Havilland plays a young and beautiful small-town gal who is unaware that fate is about to drop her on her head and launch her on a lifetime struggle to regain what she has lost. Well, you know, you frame a narrative with two world wars and you can pretty much bet that even the spunkiest of gals is going to suffer some serious heartbreak.

Jodie Norris (Olivia de Havilland) is unwilling to settle for the local boy because she's looking for a magical romance, which she finds courtesy of a square-jawed World War I pilot (John Lund) who pops into town just long enough to sell a few war bonds, give her a cynical little speech about the addictive nature of glory in battle, and knock her up before flying off to his own death. Jodie is willing to make a go of it as a single mom, but the social mores of the day force her into a ludicrous stunt that results in little Griggsy being unjustly and cruelly snatched away from her. Will he ever again look at her with eyes of love?

When you're ready for a megadose of sentimentality and a hearty sobfest about cruel, cruel fate, watch *To Each His Own* and have a good cry about your own thwarted desires.

> ⚠️ Warning Label: *This one may set up overly romantic expectations about your own impetuous flings.*

Reel to Real

In 1943, Olivia de Havilland, sick of being typecast as goody-goodys, stood up to Warner Brothers and refused a role. She was suspended for six months, and Warner demanded that she make up the lost time when her contract ran out. De Havilland sued and won. Thanks to the court's decision, known as the De Havilland Law, all performers' contracts were limited to seven years, including any suspensions, and the paternalistic studio system began crumbling. De Havilland went on to play more varied roles and won Oscars for her performances in *To Each His Own* and *The Heiress*, as well as being nominated for her role in *The Snake Pit*.

■ *Mr. Holland's Opus* (1995)
  Stars: *Richard Dreyfuss, Glenne Headley, Joseph Anderson,*
    William H. Macy, Olympia Dukakis
  Director: *Stephen Herek*
  Writer: *Patrick Sheane Duncan*

Few things make us misty like the plight of a talented, underpaid, and overworked teacher (Richard Dreyfuss as Mr. Holland). But when you pile on plot points like a shy girl discovering her uniqueness through playing the clarinet, or a boy struggling to stay in school only to have his life snuffed out before he's an adult, and then you add in a handicapped child with a powerful sense of entitlement who demands that his parents accept him and love him as is (Joseph Anderson), that mist is going to turn into a full-fledged shower of tears. And we always find that news footage of those stricken people during the quiet and frigid December Central Park memorial for John Lennon gets us all choked up, especially when they have to go and play "Imagine" over it. Throw in video of a speech by Martin Luther King, Jr., and newsreel shots of the Vietnam War to establish the time sequence and every one of our weepy buttons is pushed. And then comes the Reagan era, which is enough to make anyone wail and gnash their teeth.

But back to the actual plot. Mr. Holland is a nice guy who just wants to earn enough money teaching to take a few years off to compose his "opus," but the demands of everyday life take their toll until there he is with gray hair, a paunch, and a pink slip. The entire symphony is silenced and a man's life's work is rendered meaningless. Or is it?

Hey, if you're ready for the celebration of the sublime in the everyday, and for a virtual symphony of sobs and sniffles of your own, slip *Mr. Holland's Opus* into the VCR and let it all out.

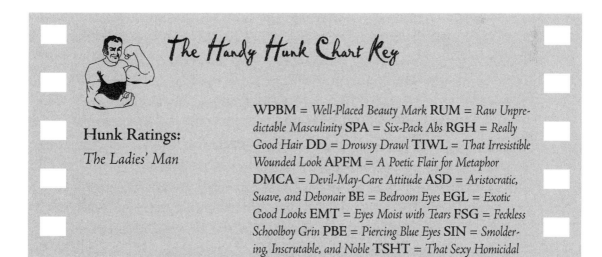

The Handy Hunk Chart Key

Hunk Ratings:
The Ladies' Man

WPBM = *Well-Placed Beauty Mark* RUM = *Raw Unpredictable Masculinity* SPA = *Six-Pack Abs* RGH = *Really Good Hair* DD = *Drowsy Drawl* TIWL = *That Irresistible Wounded Look* APFM = *A Poetic Flair for Metaphor* DMCA = *Devil-May-Care Attitude* ASD = *Aristocratic, Suave, and Debonair* BE = *Bedroom Eyes* EGL = *Exotic Good Looks* EMT = *Eyes Moist with Tears* FSG = *Feckless Schoolboy Grin* PBE = *Piercing Blue Eyes* SIN = *Smoldering, Inscrutable, and Noble* TSHT = *That Sexy Homicidal Thing* CSD = *Confidently Self-Deprecating*

The Handy Hunk Chart

Peter O'Toole   PBE, ASD, FSG, TIWL

Top Drool Pics: *Lawrence of Arabia, The Ruling Class, Beckett, The Lion in Winter, My Favorite Year*

Let's face it. Peter O'Toole is no ordinary man. After all, it's not everybody who can stay spit polished and Dippety Doo'ed in the middle of a region of the sub-Sahara known as the sun's anvil. And it's certainly not everybody who can still manage to be gallant and charming and six sheets to the wind, all at the same time. You can tie him up, tie him down, sandblast him, pummel him with wind, hang him from a cross in the parlor, or stick him on a camel in a desert, and Peter O'Toole will still emerge looking like he's just come away from a night at the opera, and maybe just had a little trouble getting a cab or something. We like that in a man. ■

Richard Burton   ASD, RUM, WPBM, FSG, DMCA

Top Drool Pics: *Beckett, Anne of the Thousand Days, The Night of the Iguana, Cleopatra, The Robe, Who's Afraid of Virginia Woolf?, Where Eagles Dare, My Cousin Rachel*

We don't know if it's the Welsh hillsides in his eyes, or the gruff music of his voice, or the fact that he popularized five o'clock shadows and hangovers as male fashion accessories, but something about Richard Burton just screams out M-A-N. And it's not everybody, you know, who can look macho in a pair of tights with his doublet unbraced while wearing a velvet beret with an enormous feather affair cascading fetchingly from the brim. And hey, if he was hunk enough to get Liz twice, he's hunk enough for us. ■

> *When it comes to pain and suffering, she's right up there with Elizabeth Taylor.*
>
> ★ Dolly Parton as Truvy Jones in *Steel Magnolias*

■ *Snow Falling on Cedars* (1999)

Stars: Ethan Hawke, Youki Kudoh, Rick Yune
Director: Scott Hicks
Writer: Ronald Bass, based on the novel by David Guterson

Ah, young love, as exquisite as a drop of rain on a cedar leaf, as exhilarating as a first kiss, as passionate as forbidden pleasure. Then comes the Dear John letter, the self-destructive behavior, and the scars that cripple us for life. Don't you just *hate* when that happens?

In this astonishingly beautiful film (check out the kaleidoscopic effect of lovemaking as seen through a mottled shower door, and the sensual depictions of nature—snowstorms never looked so cozy), a reporter named Ishmael (Ethan Hawke) has to set aside his anger and get back in touch with his youthful love for a Japanese girl named Hatsue (Youki Kudoh) in order to do the right thing. Hatsue, you see, is now married to a Japanese American man (Rick Yune) who stands accused of murdering a white man in a West Coast town post–World War II, a man against whom he had a serious grudge. The suspicion, misunderstanding, and hatred born of prejudice and bigotry, which long ago tore Ishmael and Hatsue apart and sent Ishmael off to World War II to exorcise his demons, is alive and well and living in the hearts of the all-white jury. Will Ishmael rise to the occasion and live up to the ideals of his activist/journalist father, or will he wallow in his resentment? Will the judge see to it that justice is served? And will Ethan Hawke stop already with the pained looks? 'Cause he's making us positively ache!

Watch this one when you're ready for some major sobbing and a powerful reminder of the healing power of true love.

 Warning Label: *The cinematography alone will have you weeping and wailing at the bittersweet heartache of it all.*

Freudian Slipups

One True Thing (1998)
Stars: *Meryl Streep, William Hurt, Renée Zellweger*
Director: *Carl Franklin*
Writer: *Karen Croner, based on the novel by*
Anna Quindlen

Meryl Streep was nominated for an Oscar for her portrayal of the perpetually sunny homemaker, who paints every room in the house yellow, cheerfully cooks and cleans and accepts her husband the professor's dubious excuses for coming home late, and joyfully makes Martha Stewart–like art projects out of the shards of her disappointments and mistakes. How can you resist being moved by a visibly drained and dying mother hen who is at last demanding that people stop shushing her and let her say her piece before she leaves this world?

Well, once you hear her words of wisdom to her daughter Ellen (Renée Zellweger), you'll sort of wish she'd kept her mouth shut. Oh, yes, Mom tells Ellen, she knows all about Dad's (William Hurt) philandering, hypocrisy, arrogance, and selfishness, but she's no victim. No, she's *chosen* to make concessions to a lying, cheating, conceited SOB who can't be bothered nursing his sick wife when he's got all those pretty grad students to boink. And if Ellen would only stop wearing black and feeling so dissatisfied with the limits of her own life at the moment, she could meet a nice man, have a lovely wedding, and live happily ever after in some faceless suburb somewhere. "Love what you have" glows the movie's tagline. We'd prefer to dream our dreams, whatever they may be, and to believe that true strength comes in moving beyond limited expectations of ourselves and those we love.

■ *Lorenzo's Oil* (1992)
Stars: Susan Sarandon, Nick Nolte, Kathleen Wilhoite
Director: George Miller
Writers: Nick Enright, George Miller, based on a true story

We know, we know. We avoided this movie for a long time too, because who wants to suffer along with a family whose delightful little boy develops a rare fatal disease? The trailer alone was enough to tighten our throats and blur our eyes with tears. Heck, just reading the copy on the video box had us reaching for a tissue. But *Lorenzo's Oil* is far more inspiring than it appears, justifying those gut-wrenching moments and ultimately providing hope for all of us who believe in the enormously healing power of love.

Susan Sarandon and Nick Nolte play Michaela and Augusto Odone, a solidly middle-class Italian American couple in D.C. whose lives are turned upside down when their son Lorenzo (played by several different actors and even an actress) suddenly starts acting strangely. A top neurologist breaks the bad news: Lorenzo's got adrenoleukodystrophy (ADL), an exceptionally rare genetic disease, and his prognosis is, at best, two years of agony and dementia before he inevitably succumbs. And there is no treatment.

Unable to accept such an outcome, the Odones start hitting the library to try to understand the disease and find a thread of hope somewhere. As Augusto buries himself in microbiology textbooks, Michaela spends every spare moment parenting a child who may or may not even recognize her voice anymore. And then, to the disconcertment of the medical community, the Odones work on inventing an experimental treatment derived from everyday cooking oils that may provide hope not only for their son but for boys all around the world.

Fair-minded in its portrayal of the medical community's limitations, and exquisite in its depiction of the passionate and healing love of devoted parents, *Lorenzo's Oil* will get your tear ducts flowing full force. Watch this when you want validation that loving sacrifice can pay off big time, even if we can't always have miracles on demand.

Reel to Real

The Myelin Project, founded by Augusto Odone and the late Michaela Odone to raise money for research into diseases like ADL, has financed twenty-one experiments. An estimated fourteen hundred boys and young men in the United States have this disease.

Immortal Lines from Silver Screen Sirens

No woman without a past is interesting. . . .
Women with a past make better wives.
★　Norma Shearer

We all want to perpetuate ourselves a little.
★　Jean Harlow

The only thing I regret about my past is the length of it. If I had to live my life again, I'd make the same mistakes, only sooner.
★　Tallulah Bankhead

Chapter 8

There's No Place Like Home: Dysfunctional Family Movies

Where there's smoke, there's fire. Where there's thunder, there's lightning. And wherever there's a family, there are gonna be issues—whether it's sibling rivalry, an Oedipal complex, or a smorgasbord of complexes involving the whole fam damily. No matter how much you love your next of kin, there are going to be times when the nuclear family reactor gets strained to the limits and you find yourself face-to-face with a nuclear meltdown over a plateful of pot roast and peas.

At points of critical mass like this, it's a good idea to take a deep breath, finish your dinner, and watch one of these Dysfunctional Family Movies. Maybe they'll give you a little insight into your own family fusion physics and help you to avoid critical mass.

The Whole Fam Damily

If it seems like every time you turn around there's another relative stubbing a toe on the table leg of your central conflict, and you feel like you're in danger of collapsing, watch one of these movies about families that are a lot stranger than yours. They'll help you to find patterns in the chaos, and reassure you that while you didn't choose your relatives, you probably could have done a lot worse.

■ *The Nanny* (1965)
Stars: Bette Davis, Wendy Craig, James Villiers, Jill Bennett, William Dix
Director: Seth Holt
Writer: Jimmy Sangster, based on the novel by Marryam Modell (aka Evelyn Piper)

We all know that tragic accidents can test a family's mettle and stretch the very limits of their ability to cope. But the Fanes apparently are unfamiliar with grief counseling, preferring to keep a stiff upper lip, repress all their difficult memories, and pretend everything's just hunky-dory, even though their little Joey's (William Dix) latest hobbies are drowning dolls in the bathtub and pretending to hang himself. Mom (Wendy Craig) is a weepy mess, Dad (James Villiers) is disgusted by everyone's inability to buck up and behave, and Aunt Pen's (Jill Bennett) tippling keeps her too mellowed out to suggest that perhaps they all ought to press little Joey's psychiatrist to get to the bottom of the boy's intense hatred of his kindly old Nanny (Bette Davis). Meanwhile, poor Nanny is just trying to make everybody comfy with a nice glass of tea and an understanding smile. Really, a little family counseling could go a long way toward smoothing over their transition, not to mention preventing mysterious cases of poisoning and frantic gropings for nitroglycerin pills. Talk about a creepfest! And we don't know which is scarier—the truth about what happened in the bathroom that day, or Bette Davis's eyebrows in this flick.

So if you're tired of going along with the program just because everyone thinks it's easier, *The Nanny* is a great reminder of the importance of getting to the bottom of matters before something really terrifying emerges from the shadows.

▪ *Best in Show* (2000)
  Stars: Christopher Guest, Parker Posey, Michael Hitchcock, Eugene Levy,
    Catherine O'Hara, John Michael Higgins, Michael McKean,
    Patrick Crenshaw, Jennifer Coolidge, Jane Lynch, Fred Willard
  Director: Christopher Guest
  Writers: Christopher Guest, Eugene Levy

This dark comedy from Christopher "*Spinal Tap*" and "*Waiting for Guffman*" Guest, is a movie about what happens when your dog becomes just another extension of your family dysfunction.

Four couples prepare their pets for a national canine competition. The winner will be crowned best in show—and not only will the dog be honored, but so will months of borderline psychotic behavior on the part of the champions' desperate and ego-challenged owners.

This movie is like a big metaphor for avoidance and projection issues, and all of these characters enact the drama of their central conflict through their purebred. For the Starbucks-identified yuppies Meg and Hamilton Swan (Parker Posey and Michael Hitchcock), their weimaraner has taken the place of intimacy. Gerry and Cookie's (Eugene Levy and Catherine O'Hara) terrier is a replacement for taking multiple lovers. Scott and Stefan's (John Michael Higgins and Michael McKean) shih tzu becomes their only child, and Sheri Ann and Christy's (Jennifer Coolidge and Jane Lynch) Airedale is definitely a strap-on.

In addition to affording us a hilarious pageant of the bizarre things we all do to avoid confronting our problems, this movie points out that when we make our dog a substitute for a healthy relationship, we can wind up looking really, really dorky and kind of pathetic, even if we do get best in show.

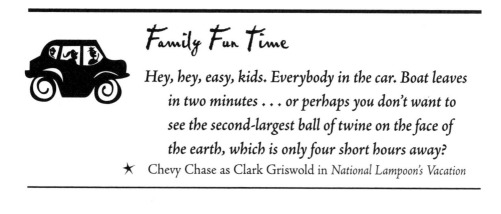

Family Fun Time

Hey, hey, easy, kids. Everybody in the car. Boat leaves in two minutes . . . or perhaps you don't want to see the second-largest ball of twine on the face of the earth, which is only four short hours away?
★ Chevy Chase as Clark Griswold in *National Lampoon's Vacation*

■ *With Six You Get Eggroll* (1968)
  Stars: Doris Day, Brian Keith, Barbara Hershey, Alice Ghostley
  Director: Howard Morris
  Writers: R. S. Allen, Harvey Bullock, based on a story by Gwen Bagni
      and Paul Dubov

Family squabbles got you down? Then you're ripe for watching this surreal time capsule about a blended family that mixes about as well as girdles and love beads and yet processes all their anger and resentment, resolves all their misunderstandings, and winds up happily sharing a suburban colonial that has the correct number of bedrooms and bathrooms.

Doris Day plays Abby McClure, a loving single mom (widowed, of course, not divorced—we're talking pre–*Ms.* magazine, you know) who runs a lumberyard and raises three kids, all without ever mussing her bubble do. Urged on by Maxine (Pat Carroll), her wacky, oversexed friend (married, naturally—because, of course, in 1968 women didn't have sex outside of marriage), Abby invites to dinner a nice single widower, Jake Iverson (Brian Keith—without the French butler and Buffy, Jodie, and Cissy this time). This, of course, leads to many zany scenes: shaggy sheepdogs running away with wigs in their mouths, harried homemakers in mud masks embarrassed in front of dinner guests, romantic secret meetings at the local burger joint, and a spur-of-the-moment decision to marry in Vegas. But our lovable single mom and dad (he's got a snotty daughter, played by a teenage Barbara Hershey) haven't gotten around to planning what comes next, much less discussing living arrangements with the kids. Hey, not a problem here.

In the name of family entertainment this movie puts a high gloss over undercurrents of anger and resentment. Watch *With Six You Get Eggroll* and have a laugh at your own tendency to deny external realities. And remember, don't try this at home.

Whatever you do, don't tell them I picked you up outside a rest room.

★ Salma Hayek as Isabel Fuentes in *Fools Rush In*

Home for the Holidays

It happens to us all once a year: the turkeys start roasting, the sleigh bells and the phone start ringing, your in-laws start whining, and before you know it, you're being carted home for the holidays. If you're being held hostage by holiday togetherness, click your heels three times, pop in one of these movies, and repeat to yourself: *There's no place like home, there's no place like home.*

Home for the Holidays (1995)
Stars: Holly Hunter, Robert Downey, Jr., Anne Bancroft, Charles Durning
Director: Jodie Foster
Writers: Chris Radant, W. D. Richter

Claudia (Holly Hunter) gets divorced, loses her job, fights with her adolescent daughter, and then she has to go home for the holidays. Watch this ultimate Thanksgiving nightmare movie when you're feeling like a skewered bird in your family's vertical roaster, and take our advice: if you can't stand the heat, stay out of the kitchen . . . and the dining room . . . and the state.

What's Cooking? (2000)
Stars: Alfre Woodard, Mercedes Ruehl, Joan Chen, Julianna Margulies,
*   Kyra Sedgwick, Maury Chaykin, Lainie Kazan*
Director: Gurinder Chadha
Writers: Paul Mayeda Berges, Gurinder Chadha

In this movie about Thanksgiving at four different ethnic American households—one Vietnamese, one Jewish, one African American, and one Hispanic—we discover that while America is indeed a multicultural mosaic, when it comes to holidays, we are united in our dysfunction. Oh, we each have our

. . . continued

own variations on the theme, just as we each have our own way of preparing the sweet potatoes and cranberries, and we each supplement the main course with our personal dishes of tamales, spring rolls, lesbian pregnancies, secret love affairs, and hidden grudges that make their way to the surface before the little thingie pops up on the turkey. Watch this one next Thanksgiving and savor your own family's banquet of craziness.

Planes, Trains and Automobiles (1987)
Stars: Steve Martin, John Candy
Director and Writer: John Hughes

It's two days before Thanksgiving and businessman Neal Page (Steve Martin) just wants to get home to his family, but he soon enters a commuter nightmare, one in which his fellow traveler, a shower-curtain-ring salesman named Del Griffith (John Candy), is the very incarnation of Jung's shadow self—kind of Neal's personal antichrist. Finally, the unfailingly polite Neal loses it and starts ranting about Del's personal habits and insufferable babbling. But just then he sees the pain in Del's eyes, and he begins to realize that sometimes fate puts people in our path so that we can grow beyond our own limitations and recognize that we're all part of a human family, even if some of our relatives make us want to jump out at twelve thousand feet. This Thanksgiving-themed movie will remind you to practice love and acceptance, but draw your boundaries too.

Home Alone (1990)
Stars: Macauley Culkin, Catherine O'Hara, Joe Pesci, Daniel Stern
Director: Chris Columbus
Writer: John Hughes

Adorable eight-year-old Kevin McCallister (Macauley Culkin) is accidentally left behind when his family leaves for a Christmas in Paris. At first he's thrilled to have the place to himself, but eventually, because he's eight and

. . . *continued*

hasn't developed any independence issues yet, he longs for his family to return home, which they do, just in time to sit down to a big Christmas dinner together. Watch this movie when you want to remind yourself how great Christmas would be if you were just willing to remain forever a child, and not insist on things like respect for your individuality or adult independence.

It's a Wonderful Life (1946)
Stars: *James Stewart, Donna Reed, Lionel Barrymore*
Director: *Frank Capra*
Writers: *Philip Van Doren Stern, Frances Goodrich, Albert Hackett, Frank Capra*

There are a lot of holiday traditions we all wish we could toss out with the rotting jack-o'-lantern: Uncle Mervin's loud and off-color jokes that the kids want explained to them, Grandma's burned yams, Cousin Sophie's insistence that you're stirring the gravy with entirely the wrong spoon. No wonder it's so blissful to pop in that feel-good classic *It's a Wonderful Life* and escape to a world of honorable men, a loving community, and guardian angels who turn the worst disasters into life-affirming celebrations. Yes, you've seen it a million times, but some holiday traditions are worth repeating.

Dysfunctional Family Jewels

Nobody means what they say on Thanksgiving,
Mom. You know that. That's what the day's
supposed to be all about, right? Torture.
   ★   Holly Hunter as Claudia in *Home for the Holidays*

We don't have to like each other. We're family.
   ★   Holly Hunter as Claudia in *Home for the Holidays*

■ *Addams Family Values* (1993)
 Stars: *Anjelica Huston, Raul Julia, Christopher Lloyd, Joan Cusack,*
    Christina Ricci, Carol Kane, Christine Baranski, Jimmy Workman
 Director: *Barry Sonnenfeld*
 Writers: *Paul Rudnick, based on characters by Charles Addams*

America's kookiest family greets a new addition to the household and proves that when it comes to dysfunctional family issues, even ghoulish creatures who spawn in the dark and damp recesses of the graveyard, cut the heads off roses, and shun the light of day are no different than all the rest of us.

When Morticia (Anjelica Huston) and Gomez (Raul Julia) bring home their new son Pubert, their other children, Pugsley (Jimmy Workman) and Wednesday (Christina Ricci), stage a lethal enactment of their sibling rivalry issues. To cope with the emotional and structural fallout, Morticia and Gomez hire a nanny, Debbie Jellinsky (Joan Cusack), who turns out to be a black widow who marries rich men and then murders them. Debbie ships Pugsley and Wednesday off to a camp headed by two overgrown cheerleaders, Gary Granger (Peter MacNicol) and Becky Martin-Granger (Christine Baranski), and marries the hapless Uncle Fester (Christopher Lloyd). In the course of the conflagration that follows, all the skeletons of American family dysfunction come rattling out of the closet. As a consequence of this test of their familial bonds, the Addamses discover that while they may prefer thorns over blossoms, and nightmares over pleasant dreams, when it comes to loving one another, they are a functional family dream come true.

This is a great movie to watch when things start getting spooky in your domestic arena and you need to remember that no matter how creepy and kooky, mysterious and ooky, things look on the surface, underneath it all, you're still family.

 Dysfunctional Family Jewels

To all that binds a family together. To mirth, to merriment, to manslaughter.
 ★   Raul Julia as Gomez in *Addams Family Values*

---

*You have gone too far. You have married Fester, you have de-
stroyed his spirit, you have taken him from us. All that I could
forgive. But Debbie . . . pastels?*

★ Anjelica Huston as Morticia in *Addams Family Values*

Morticia: Do you remember our honeymoon?
Gomez: That glorious cruise! No calls.
Morticia: No cares.
Gomez: No survivors.

★ from *Addams Family Values*

■ *What's Eating Gilbert Grape?* (1993)

Stars: Johnny Depp, Juliette Lewis, Leonardo DiCaprio
Director: Lasse Hallström
Writer: Peter Hedges

Johnny Depp plays Gilbert Grape, the young son of a morbidly obese and depressed mother who hasn't left the house in seven years. Gilbert's life is further complicated by his developmentally disabled brother Arnie (Leonardo DiCaprio), for whom he is the primary caregiver. Arnie is basically a good and lovable kid, but he's got a wild streak that crops up occasionally, prompting Arnie to do stuff like climb to the top of a water tower and try to jump off. And guess who gets to talk him down? You got it. Every time poor Gilbert turns around somebody has a boo-boo that Gilbert has to kiss and make better.

Sound familiar? We think overachieving daughters of dysfunctional families everywhere can find a lot to relate to in this story of poor Gilbert Grape, who has so many chores around the house that he can't find the time to come of age or have a love life. Watch *What's Eating Gilbert Grape?* when you're feeling overburdened, and remember that the heavier your baggage, the more important it is to find some good strong beams to shore up the floorboards.

Sibling Rivalry

There's no doubt about it. When it comes to mom and dad's attention, we all have a spoiled three-year-old inside of us who doesn't want to share. When you're feeling cheated because of what the stork drug in, watch one of these Sibling Rivalry Movies that remind us of what can happen when we don't make peace with the competition.

■ **Dead Ringer** (1964)
Stars: Bette Davis, Karl Malden, Peter Lawford
Director: Paul Henreid
Writers: Albert Beich, Oscar Millard, based on the story
 "Dead Pigeon" by Rian James

In this classic sibling rivalry flick, Bette Davis plays Edith "Edie" Phillips, a disappointed woman who loses the man she loves to her twin sister, and turns to a life of smoky barrooms and jazz quintets to avoid confronting her sibling rivalry issues. Bette Davis also plays Margaret, Edith's coldhearted identical twin, who long ago stole Edith's boyfriend, although she never really loved him, and has now murdered him for his fortune. Oh, and she wears really expensive Schiaparelli gowns and diamond brooches the size of your fist, while Edith wears off-the-rack Dacron polyester and sensible shoes.

There are so many sibling betrayals in this movie that it's hard to put your finger on which one actually puts Edie over the edge. Is it when soon-to-be-evicted Edie visits long-estranged Margaret and has to watch her flaunt her extravagant lifestyle? Is it when Edie discovers that Margaret had not only stolen her beau those many years ago, but tricked him into marrying her by lying about being pregnant? Is it when Edie realizes that said beau had, like her, spent decades feeling miserable because of Margaret's selfishness? Or is it just that Margaret is an insufferable megabitch egomaniac who has been making Edie positively buggy since the day they emerged together from their mother's womb?

Okay, so Margaret is the quintessential evil twin. But Edie's got a lot going for her, and stealing her sister's identity doesn't seem like the best way to work through her feelings of jealousy. This movie is a masterfully crafted cinematic metaphor for our deepest homicidal instincts toward our siblings, and shows us the horrible consequences of exacting your revenge on your sister, even if she totally deserves it.

■ *The Cement Garden* (1993)
Stars: Andrew Robertson, Charlotte Gainsbourg
Director and Writer: Andrew Birkin

There's nothing like an incestuous love affair between two adolescent and orphaned siblings to cure your why-is-my-sibling-such-a-freak blues and make us all feel a little better about our own dysfunctional families of origin.

When their brutish father dies of a heart attack while cementing over the family garden, and their sainted mother perishes from a mysterious ailment, Jack (Andrew Robertson) and Julie (Charlotte Gainsbourg) are left to care for their two younger siblings and each other. Free from the constraints of the adult world, like sexual taboos and customary burial procedures, the children construct a world in the image of their collective fantasies, which include the usual hobgoblins of gender bending, boundary bleeding, and total lack of good housekeeping skills. Which just goes to show you, it's good to love your sibling, just not too much.

Watch this movie when you're feeling entombed in the emotional cement of your own sibling relationships. After spending a couple of hours in this dysfunctional family's basement, your own psychological crawl space will feel like a breath of fresh air.

■ *Hanging Up* (2000)
Stars: Meg Ryan, Walter Matthau, Diane Keaton, Lisa Kudrow,
    Cloris Leachman
Director: Diane Keaton
Writer: Delia Ephron, based on her novel

Theoretically, dutiful daughter Eve (Meg Ryan) has two sisters to share the burden of caring for an aging parent, but for all their accessibility by phone and sympathetic tones, they never seem able to actually *do* anything to help out. Every five minutes Eve takes yet another call from her increasingly senile dad (Walter Matthau), who can't find the switch on his lamp and doesn't understand why he can't order up moo goo gai pan from his locked ward in the nursing home. But Eve can't convince either her narcissistic, flaky sister Maddy (Lisa Kudrow) or her narcissistic, hypercompetent sister Georgia (Diane Keaton) to put their lives on hold for just five minutes and consider maybe helping out. Eve is in perpetual panic mode, desperate to please her first big client for her events-planning business, who suddenly wants her to hire Georgia to be the inspirational speaker at her party because *everybody* loves Georgia, you know. And somehow Eve has gotten suckered into giving Maddy's Saint Bernard seizure medication four times a day.

If you're the underappreciated middle child, literally or metaphorically, *Hanging Up* will reassure you that being the dutiful daughter is a wonderful thing, but that maybe you need to screen your calls more often and get someone else to pitch in.

■ *Twin Falls Idaho* (1999)
Stars: *Michael Polish, Mark Polish, Michele Hicks, Teresa Hill*
Director: *Michael Polish*
Writer: *Michael Polish, Mark Polish*

Okay, we know, your sibling is driving you nuts, but just imagine if the two of you were attached at the hip—literally.

Francis and Blake Falls (Michael Polish and Mark Polish) are Siamese twins who live in a single-occupancy, rent-by-the-hour, urban allegory on the wrong side of town. While the two brothers share one tiny room and a few vital organs, their similarities stop there. Blake is healthy and vital and outgoing. He's good with a witty one-liner and has a boyish vulnerability that really wows the ladies, despite his inconvenient and somewhat unsightly fraternal appendage. Francis, on the other hand, has crossed the line from vulnerable into pathetic. He's sickly, shy, and girls have little use for him.

Blake and Francis's stark and insular lives become complicated when Blake and a kittenish hooker, Penny (Michele Hicks), fall in love, and just as Blake is beginning to enjoy a full life as a man, Francis falls ill and it becomes apparent that one brother is going to have to die so that the other might live.

This is a great movie to watch when you're being annoyed by your inconvenient fraternal appendage and need to remember that no matter how needy he may become, he ain't heavy, he's your brother.

Mom Issues

The vision of the metaphorical mom, that all-suffering, all-knowing, all-powerful lady with unconditional love in her heart and a really heavy frying pan in her hand, has sent us all scurrying for a comfy couch, comfort food, and a cinematic escape at one time or another. Fortunately, filmmakers seem to be a group with a lot of mom issues too, because there are acres of footage on the subject. So the next time you find yourself in the maternal frying pan, pop in one of these Mom Issue Movies and get out of the kitchen.

■ *Drop Dead Gorgeous* (1999)
    Stars: Kirsten Dunst, Ellen Barkin, Allison Janney, Denise Richards,
       Kirstie Alley
    Director: Michael Patrick Jann
    Writer: Lona Williams

This mock-umentary, a kind of *Spinal Tap* of the teen beauty circuit, is about a small-town pageant in which would-be teen princesses compete to win back the love of emotionally absent mothers and wind up getting blown up, food-poisoned, and cheated out of their shot at national competition. Now that'll make you think twice about doing anything just because your mother told you to.

Amber Atkins (Kirsten Dunst), a talented tapper from the trailer park, and Becky Ann Leeman (Denise Richards), the town debutante, compete for the crown of Miss Teen Princess largely to satisfy the unrequited pageant dreams of their narcissistic, hypercompetitive moms. Gladys Leeman (Kirstie Alley) is a voracious former beauty queen who stole the crown out from under the more beautiful but more economically challenged

Annette Atkins (Ellen Barkin) years before. Now, years later, with many Marlboro Lights and Budweiser cans under her mother's bridge, Amber returns as her mother's redeemer to take the crown back to the trailer park where it belongs.

This movie is about rich versus poor, good versus evil, and about the dangerous potential of trailer park electrical wiring and foreign-made swan floats. It's also a very good cautionary tale about the trouble we can all get into when we devote our heart and soul and tap shoes to make Mom's dream come true instead of our own.

Be Careful What You Wish For

And so, dear Lord, it is with deep sadness that we turn over to you this young woman, whose dream to ride on a giant swan resulted in her death. Maybe it is your way of telling us . . . to buy American.

★ Richard Ooms as the pastor in *Drop Dead Gorgeous*

I'd have good strong roots in a town like Mount Rose, a solid Christian trunk, and long, leafy branches for handicapped children to use as shelter.

★ Denise Richards as Becky Ann Leeman in *Drop Dead Gorgeous*

Hi. I'm Amber Atkins, and I am signing up 'cause two of my favorite persons in the world competed in pageants: my mom and Diane Sawyer. Of course, I want to end up more like Diane Sawyer than my mom.

★ Kirsten Dunst as Amber Atkins in *Drop Dead Gorgeous*

▪ *Psycho* (1960)
Stars: Anthony Perkins, Janet Leigh, Vera Miles, John Gavin, Martin Balsam
Director: Alfred Hitchcock
Writers: Robert Bloch, Joseph Stefano

Sometimes the most dangerous mom issues aren't *your* mom issues at all, but somebody else's—that's the case in this classic Hitchcock movie. The weirdness begins when reluctant larcenist Marion Crane (Janet Leigh) checks in to the Bates Motel for the night, after stealing forty thousand dollars to finance a new life with her divorced boyfriend. But while Marion has enough sense to come in out of the rain, she doesn't stop to consider that a darkened roadhouse with twelve rooms and twelve vacancies, run by a beakish mama's boy called Norman (Anthony Perkins), who has a facial tic and a master key and stuffs birds for kicks, is probably not a good place to spend the night.

Of course, we don't think Marion is alone when it comes to suspending her better judgment about shy and vulnerable men/children who appeal to her maternal instincts. But as *Psycho* so vividly illustrates, when a grown man who still lives at home tells you his best friend is his mother, it's probably best to keep moving on down the road, or at least lock the bathroom door before you step into the shower.

▪ *The Anniversary* (1968)
Stars: Bette Davis, Sheila Hancock, Jack Hedley, James Cossins, Christian Roberts
Director: Roy Ward Baker
Writer: Jimmy Sangster, based on the play by Bill MacIlwraith

She's got tobacco-stained teeth, a paisley-shaped satin eyepatch glued onto her right eyesocket and two pounds of blue eyeshadow above the false eyelashes on the other, a drink in one hand and a cigarette in the other, and red talons reaching out toward you. Yes, Mama Taggart (Bette Davis) is indeed the original Freudian homicidal mother, delighting in the total destruction of her children's psyches. And no one plays the megabitch from hell better than Bette Davis.

The vicious Mrs. Taggart tells the ugliest of lies just to punish her children for conceiving of possibly standing up to her, and smiles as she imagines being able to place them into her cabinet along with her other possessions, like the inanimate objects she wishes they were. "I've had three chits of my own, only three, I grant you, Karen," Mama tells one daughter-in-law. "But natural good manners told me when to put the plug in." And boy, she loves a fight: "That's more like my daughter-in-law! Down on all fours, spitting away, with her whiskers quivering."

Believe us, you'll get the itch to hold up a crucifix or search for a silver bullet after just a few minutes of this banquet of dysfunction, and don't be surprised if you recognize some of the unhealthy reactions to Mom's narcissism, even if they are blown up to big-screen proportions. This is a great one to watch when you need a nudge to start changing your part in the family dynamic and drawing some boundaries with your own mom.

Freudian Slipups

Hush (1998)
Stars: Jessica Lange, Gwyneth Paltrow, Johnathon Schaech
Director and Writer: Jonathan Darby

We know, she's impossible, that mother-in-law of yours. But believe us, a little bossiness about your holiday plans and unsolicited advice about how to raise your kids is nothing compared to the behavior of Jessica Lange in this outrageously over-the-top thriller. Helen (Gwyneth Paltrow) doesn't realize that behind the sweet smile and honey voice of mother-in-law Martha Baring (Jessica Lange) is a viper ready to suck the lifeblood out of her. We wince at Helen's naïveté at first, then get downright irritated at her lack of boundaries. But frankly, should we ever find ourselves held hostage by an Old Testament–quoting, crocheting madwoman who is ready to shoot us up with a lethal dose of morphine after we've just given birth sans epidural, we hope we'd be a little less revenge obsessed than Helen. Despite her near-death experience, she skips the call to 911 (as does her dopey husband, played by Johnathon Schaech) so that she can mentally torture Martha over scrambled eggs in the sunny kitchen the next morning. Listen, getting the last word and opening hubby's eyes once and for all has its appeal, but so does quality medical care postpartum.

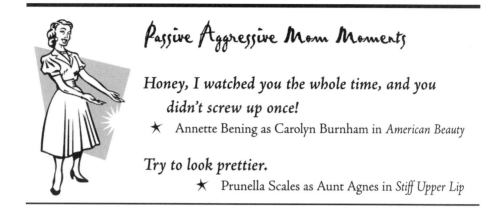

Passive Aggressive Mom Moments

Honey, I watched you the whole time, and you didn't screw up once!
  ★ Annette Bening as Carolyn Burnham in *American Beauty*

Try to look prettier.
  ★ Prunella Scales as Aunt Agnes in *Stiff Upper Lip*

Father Issues

Let's face it, on some level we're all still searching for dad's love and approval, even though we're fully grown and have become parents ourselves. Some of us become classic overachievers, working day and night to get our metaphorical father within to say he's proud of us, even though we flubbed the word *chiaroscuro* in that fourth-grade spelling bee. Some of us fall in love with a guy just like the guy who married good old mom, and some of us look to elected officials to satisfy that craving for a loving and protective patriarch. However you've chosen to cope with the big kahuna in your inner realm, these Father Issue Movies will help you to make peace with the dear old dad within, and without.

▪ **Cider House Rules** (1999)
Stars: Tobey Maguire, Charlize Theron, Michael Caine, Jane Alexander
Director: Lasse Hallström
Writer: John Irving, based on his novel

It's interesting that one of the most relevant dad issue movies begins in an orphanage, but it just goes to show you, when it comes to father issues, you can run, but you can't hide. Homer Wells (Tobey Maguire) is born in an orphanage/abortion clinic in Maine in the

1930s. Homer is adopted twice, but it never quite sticks and he winds up being raised by the hospital's physician, Dr. Wilbur Larch (Michael Caine). No biological father ever loved a son more, however, and Wilbur teaches Homer everything he knows about caring for mothers and children. Father and son work side by side, healing the sick, delivering unwanted babies, and raising their "kings of New England" with love and concern.

Homer follows in his father's footsteps with two notable exceptions: he doesn't share his father's ether addiction or his pro-choice stance. Homer, therefore, leaves his unlicensed medical career behind him and goes to live as a farmhand in a cider house, which breaks his father's heart. Will Homer return to Maine and make peace with his father before he dies? Or will he remain in exile, wasting his considerable talents pressing fruit into pulp?

This intelligent movie asks very relevant questions about what it means both to be and to have a father. Watch it when you're feeling fed up with paternal expectations and need to find a common ground where you and dad can meet and write a set of cider house rules that you both can live with.

■ *Nixon* (1995)
Stars: Anthony Hopkins, Joan Allen
Director: Oliver Stone
Writers: Steven J. Rivele, Christopher Wilkinson, Oliver Stone

We Americans have a national father complex: we always want our authorities to be some fatherly-looking guy who is going to dispense justice from his hallowed position on high. We want our men of power to be the perfect patriarchs, but *Nixon* is one of those movies that urges us to get a grip and stop the insanity.

Oliver Stone's Richard Nixon (Anthony Hopkins) is the apotheosis of the patriarchal president, who wields unquestionable power, heeds no authority but his own, and pays the wages of power with twelve-year-old scotch and bad performance in the bedroom. Leave it to Oliver Stone to lay it on thick and extra long, but *Nixon* is a good reminder of what can happen when we project our father issues on presidents, or directors for that matter, and grant them absolute power in the cutting room.

▪ *Roger & Me* (1989)
Stars: Michael Moore, James Bond, Pat Boone, Bob Eubanks
Director and Writer: Michael Moore

Roger & Me is an eighties documentary about trying to track down General Motors chairman Roger Smith to confront him about the devastating effect that the Flint GM factory closing has had on Flint, Michigan, where forty thousand jobs were lost. Throughout the film, the nebbishy Michael Moore interviews the locals and chronicles Flint's downfall. He asks the hard questions, like what responsibility does a corporation have to the town, and is he a winter or a summer. Unfortunately, Moore never gets to ask them of the local patriarch, who is exceedingly well insulated from the proles. This movie is a darkly humorous reminder that big business is not just like dear old dad. Corporations do not always know best, and they can't be trusted to take out the garbage.

Only six months after opening, Autoworld closed due to a lack of visitors. I guess it was like expecting a million people a year to go to New Jersey to Chemicalworld, or a million people going to Valdez, Alaska, for Exxonworld. Some people just don't like to celebrate human tragedy while on vacation.

★ Michael Moore in *Roger & Me*

▪ *The Mosquito Coast* (1986)
Stars: Harrison Ford, River Phoenix, Helen Mirren
Director: Peter Weir
Writer: Paul Schrader, based on the novel by Paul Theroux

Dad sure is an iconoclast, with his progressive views on politics, his quirky sense of priorities, and his Hawaiian shirts and modified Gilligan hats. Ya gotta love him, really. But as Charlie (River Phoenix), the eldest son of Allie Fox (Harrison Ford), comes to discover, filial love—and loyalty—can blind us to the crippling character flaws of our parents and lead us down a garden path into a thicket that's difficult to escape from.

Allie, tired of practical matters like making money and doing jobs for which he was hired, dreams of nobler pursuits, like, say, becoming a modern Prometheus bringing ice to noble savages in the depths of the rain forest in some obscure corner of the world known as the Mosquito Coast. His hypersupportive wife (Helen Mirren, billed only as "Mother," which is what hubby calls her) dutifully packs up the children, yards of sunny yellow material for clothing, and plenty of sunblock. It's up to Charlie to acknowledge that this emperor not only has no clothes, but no gasoline, working outboard, or foul-weather gear. And considering that Allie has just built his little Robinson Crusoe outpost in the middle of the floodplain, Charlie is going to have to launch a coup unless he wants his family to end up underneath a pile of mud.

Watch *The Mosquito Coast* when you sense you've been making far too many excuses for someone who is just a little too big for his Old Navy cargo shorts, and remind yourself that your own dreams, no matter how simple, count just as much as his do.

Why do things get worse and worse? They don't have to. They could get better and better. We accept that things fall apart.
★ Harrison Ford as Allie Fox in *The Mosquito Coast*

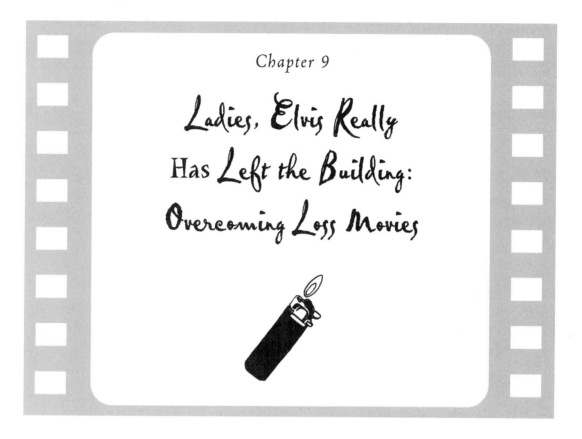

Chapter 9

Ladies, Elvis Really Has Left the Building: Overcoming Loss Movies

It's one of the fundamental truths of the human experience: nobody likes change, and everybody fears the unknown. But there are a lot of valuable lessons to be learned from loss, and chaos can be a creative force in service of a better order—even if it does mean we'll have to repaint the whole house once the dust settles.

Whether it's the loss of a loved one or the disappearance of a cherished dream, at some point we've all got to face the fact that Elvis really has left the building, and we're going to have to move on. So if you've been stomping your foot ever since the last Sun City Session, and your Bic lighter is running out of fuel but you still haven't heard an encore, watch one of these Overcoming Loss Movies about people who have had to learn to let go or pay the high price of dwelling in the past. Maybe then it'll be a little easier to check out of your own heartbreak hotel.

■ *Passion Fish* (1992)
Stars: Mary McDonnell, Alfre Woodard
Director and Writer: John Sayles

Mary-Alice (Mary McDonnell), a successful soap star, has recently become paralyzed from the waist down, and is back in her hometown along the bayou learning to adjust to life in a wheelchair. But unlike most of our screen heroines who overcome life-altering disasters with good grace and humility, Mary-Alice is a real bitch about the whole thing. She's ungrateful, overly possessive of the remote control, and more often than not has her hand glued to a wine bottle. Oh, and she doesn't bathe or change clothes very often either. She is, in fact, the picture of everything that a self-sacrificing, all-enduring woman is not supposed to be in the face of tragedy.

And this is why we love Mary-Alice. Even though she is paralyzed from the waist down, she finds a way to plant her feet defiantly in the dirt and flip the bird at the inevitable. She says no to physical therapy, upper-body strength, good nutrition, and the outside world—no to friends, nurses, proper hygiene, and sobriety. And then she meets Chantelle (Alfre Woodard), an indomitable nurse's aide with a ten-mile stare and the scars to match, who won't take no for an answer.

When you're feeling debilitated and helpless, and more than just a little pissed off, watch *Passion Fish* and shake your fist at the facts, and then open up your hands, accept the inevitable, and move on.

World-Class Wrecks

And on a cold winter's night, Horace, you can snuggle up to your cash register. It's a little lumpy but it rings!

★ Barbra Streisand as Dolly Levi in *Hello, Dolly!*

■ *Not Without My Daughter* (1991)
Stars: Sally Field, Alfred Molina, Sheila Rosenthal, Roshan Seth
Director: Brian Gilbert
Writer: William Hoffer, based on the book by Betty Mahmoody and
   William Hoffer

Moody Mahmoody (Alfred Molina) sure seemed like a regular fella, even if he did come from a very conservative Iranian family. But American Betty Mahmoody (Sally Field) made a bad misstep when she agreed to a trip back home to meet her husband's family while a revolution was brewing ("C'mon, Betty," he says. "It's not such a big deal." Yeah, famous last words). Indeed, Betty senses this visit might not go so smoothly when Moody's family arrives at the airport, swoops down on her husband and daughter, and carries them off gleefully, leaving her to lug the suitcases. The relatives start talking to Moody in Farsi, and judging by his facial expressions and the tone of their voices, they probably aren't discussing the local museum schedules.

When Betty's husband mutates into a fanatical revolutionary and she realizes she's stuck in a country that doesn't hold American homemakers and potential divorcées in high esteem, it's time for her to start letting go of her illusions, no matter how painful that may be, and start imagining a new future.

Watch this when you've come to realize that your man isn't who you thought he was. Then assess what is essential and leave the rest behind.

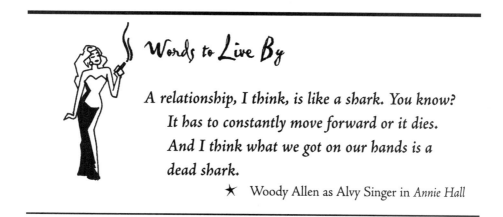

Words to Live By

A relationship, I think, is like a shark. You know?
It has to constantly move forward or it dies.
And I think what we got on our hands is a
dead shark.
   ★ Woody Allen as Alvy Singer in *Annie Hall*

■ *Holiday Affair* (1949)

Stars: Janet Leigh, Robert Mitchum, Wendell Corey
Director: Don Hartman
Writer: Isobel Lennart, based on the story "Christmas Gift" by John D. Weaver

Come the holidays, a lot of us get sentimental and find ourselves dwelling in an idealized past filled with Norman Rockwell scenarios, perfect love affairs unmarred by human frailty, and hearty meals that fill our stomachs but not the fat cells in our thighs.

Alright, so maybe we tend to paint the past with a happy brush, which can make it difficult to let go of what was and embrace what is. This is a truth that bereaved widow and single mom Connie Ennis (Janet Leigh) is reminded of when she meets the delightfully happy-go-lucky Steve Mason (Robert Mitchum). Connie is unsettled by Steve's frankness about her situation, and she bristles at the suggestion that maybe she ought not marry her ho-hum fiancé Carl (Wendell Corey), move to the suburbs, and pretend that she and her son aren't living in the shadow of the ghost of her idealized late husband. But Connie and Steve keep bumping into each other by accident—or is it fate?—and despite Connie's best attempts to make Steve a footnote in her personal memory book, he continues to reappear in her life like some Buddha on the road, annoying her with simple truths that lay bare her fundamental psychological conflicts.

But as is often the case, what we don't *want* to hear is exactly what we *need* to hear. And just as you can be sure that a postwar holiday season release will center on the Christmas message of renewal and hope, you can rest easy knowing that Connie will finally be honest with herself, put her losses behind her, and embrace her future.

In need of a little nudge to get on with it already? Then snuggle up with *Holiday Affair* and a cozy blanket, make yourself a nice cup of tea, and promise yourself to open a new chapter already. You'll be glad you did.

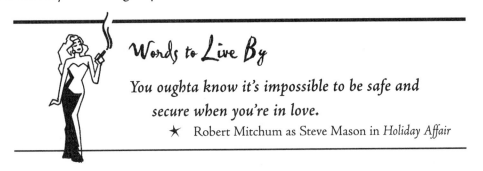

Words to Live By

You oughta know it's impossible to be safe and
secure when you're in love.
★ Robert Mitchum as Steve Mason in *Holiday Affair*

The Handy Hunk Chart Key

Hunk Ratings:

All-American Bad Boys

WPBM = *Well-Placed Beauty Mark* RUM = *Raw Unpredictable Masculinity* SPA = *Six-Pack Abs* RGH = *Really Good Hair* DD = *Drowsy Drawl* TIWL = *That Irresistible Wounded Look* APFM = *A Poetic Flair for Metaphor* DMCA = *Devil-May-Care Attitude* ASD = *Aristocratic, Suave, and Debonair* BE = *Bedroom Eyes* EGL = *Exotic Good Looks* EMT = *Eyes Moist with Tears* FSG = *Feckless Schoolboy Grin* PBE = *Piercing Blue Eyes* SIN = *Smoldering, Inscrutable, and Noble* TSHT = *That Sexy Homicidal Thing* CSD = *Confidently Self-Deprecating*

The Handy Hunk Chart

Jared Leto

WPBM, RGH, TIWL, SIN

Top Drool Pics: *Basil, American Psycho, Girl, Interrupted, Sunset Strip, Requiem for a Dream*

When Jared Leto first entered our consciousness it was as that adorable and insouciant Jordan Catalano in the TV series *My So-Called Life*. Jordan was like the apotheosis of our high school bad boy dreams: great hair that's always in his face; deep, dark, largely vacant eyes; and a really well placed birthmark. Jared Leto as Jordan Catalano was like male marzipan. But then Jared grew up and started appearing in Merchant-Ivory–inspired period pieces and pronouncing florid sentences with multiple clauses in a relatively convincing British accent. And it's not everybody who can look haunted and excruciatingly beautiful in a pair of those bizarre high-waisted Victorian

. . . continued

trousers. Jared Leto started to look startlingly like something we never expected: a nice boy that you'd love to take home to mother. What's a girl to do? But then, just as we began to get alarmed, *Requiem for a Dream* came out, featuring a Jared Leto who is once again a charming miscreant in need of reform, with the obligatory forelock of hair in his eyes, and all was once again right with the world. Although we have to admit, we do sort of miss those snug, high-waisted period trousers and that cute little Victorian accent. Maybe Jared is helping us acknowledge once and for all that bad boys can become good boys, and still manage to be sexy. Now wouldn't that be a relief! ■

Paul Newman

PBE, RUM, DMCA, FSG

Top Drool Pics: *Somebody Up There Likes Me, Hud, Cool Hand Luke, The Hustler, Butch Cassidy and the Sundance Kid, The Color of Money, The Sting*

There are hunks, and then there are HUNKS, and then there's Paul Newman, who took the image of the cinematic bad boy and elevated it to the level of religion. Those aren't just blue eyes, those are windows to heaven. That's not just some guy walking down the highway, that's the swaggering cocksure embodiment of male sexuality. That's not just a hard-boiled egg sliding down a convict's throat, that's a metaphor for the invincibility of the human spirit. And that's not just salad dressing, that's the vinaigrette of human kindness. C'mon—the man makes seventy-five look sexy. Paul Newman is a hunk for all seasons. ■

■ *The Sweet Hereafter* (1997)
Stars: Ian Holm, Maury Chaykin, Sarah Polley
Director: Atom Egoyan
Writer: Russell Banks, Atom Egoyan

The Sweet Hereafter is a movie about how we cope when the worst has already happened. A school bus accident claims the lives of fourteen children in a small Canadian hill town, transforming the tiny burg into a modern-day Hamelin after the piper has led all of the children away. An ambulance-chasing Mitchell Stevens (Ian Holm) arrives to convince the bereaved parents to sue the bus company and recover damages for the lives of their children. Some families are willing, some are reluctant, as a schism grows in the town between those who can accept that terrible accidents happen, make their peace, and move on, and those who must place blame and remain mired in anger.

This movie is a series of portraits of ordinary, small-town people dealing with epic grief, and teaches us all something about human resilience, and the unique gifts that the acceptance of terrible loss has to offer.

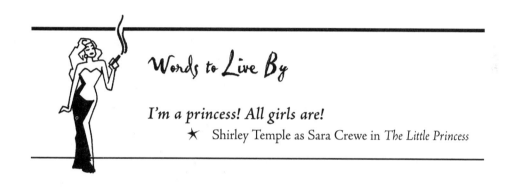

Words to Live By

I'm a princess! All girls are!
★ Shirley Temple as Sara Crewe in *The Little Princess*

■ *Where the Heart Is* (2000)

Stars: Natalie Portman, Ashley Judd, Stockard Channing, James Frain
Director: Matt Williams
Writers: Lowell Ganz, Babaloo Mandel, based on the novel by Billie Letts

Left literally barefoot and pregnant in Sequoia, Oklahoma, Novalee Nation (Natalie Portman) secretly takes shelter in the local Wal-Mart and awaits her baby's birth in Aisle 5 one stormy night. You'd think the weight of her boyfriend's betrayal and abandonment would leave Novalee curled up in a corner somewhere, but being seventeen and possessed of a relentless can-do attitude, our gal makes the most of what little life has to offer a trailer park angel with a heart of pure gold. Before you can say, "Someone take that Queen Amidala merchandise off the rack or it's gonna ruin the interior Wal-Mart shot," Novalee has become a national sweetheart for giving birth in the Wal-Mart, and has attracted a collection of lovable oddballs (Ashley Judd, Stockard Channing, and James Frain) who help her out. Her new friends offer her unconditional acceptance, a place to live, and a young and flexible buckeye tree that serves as a metaphor for her ability to bend with the wind while reaching for the sky.

Nothing knocks Novalee flat, not even for a moment, even though she only weighs about eighty pounds soaking wet. When random tragedies pop up like gophers, the preternaturally poised Novalee walks tall, content with her supportive (well, technically speaking, codependent) beau, newly inherited plot of land, recently won photojournalism award, and that upsweep and little black dress that makes her look like the Audrey Hepburn of the panhandle.

Now it's true that this movie offers little more than surface calm. Frankly, we found it easier to believe that an OB-GYN nurse (the Judd character) could get—whoops!—accidentally pregnant six times than that Portman—blessed with flawless skin, pristine bone structure, a supermodel bod, and a headful of chunky highlights that warm up her brunette tresses—could hail from Lower Horsetail. And really, *Where the Heart Is* offers an overly bright picture of what it's like to rebuild your life and esteem after a tremendous loss. But if your faith in humankind has been shaken lately, and you are willing to overlook enough implausibilities to fill the shelves of every Wal-Mart in the land, *Where the Heart Is* may be just the right flick for you. It reassures us that while we can't control the twists and turns of circumstance, we can be sure that if we care for our buckeye tree with love, it will eventually bear fruit.

▪ *The Hurricane* (1999)

Stars: Denzel Washington, Vicellous Reon Shannon
Director: Norman Jewison
Writers: Armyan Bernstein, Dan Gordon, based on the books The 16th Round *by Rubin "Hurricane" Carter and Lazarus and* The Hurricane *by Sam Chaiton and Terry Swinton*

So what would a prizewinning boxer be afraid of? "Doors opening," says imprisoned Rubin "The Hurricane" Carter to a young admirer, "the light outside . . . and you." Well, he also fears the system of justice in America and in Paterson, New Jersey, in particular. On a more universal note, The Hurricane fears what we all do when we feel powerless: embracing hope when it's so much safer and easier to give up.

Rubin Carter (Denzel Washington) has spent most of his life in prison or detention centers for the crime of being in the wrong place at the wrong time, with the wrong color skin ("Innocence," he explains, "is a highly overrated commodity"). When he is befriended by a teenage boy, Lazarus "Lesra" Martin (Vicellous Reon Shannon), who discovered the joy of reading for the first time when he read The Hurricane's autobiography, the ex-fighter faces a new challenge, one that doesn't wear satin shorts. Lesra wants to reopen The Hurricane's case and his heart as well, but his hero has made a home of his prison and he's not sure he can open the door to hope one more time when it seems inevitable that it will slam shut in his face again. To Lesra and Lesra's mentors he writes, "Please find it in your hearts not to weaken me with your love." Not a demand to make of idealistic youth with time on their hands, who are more than ready to rise to the challenge of winning a hopeless case.

This movie reminds us that while expectations set us up for disappointments, spending too much time coping and not enough time hoping is its own kind of prison. *The Hurricane* will prove a powerful catalyst to get you thinking outside of your own box.

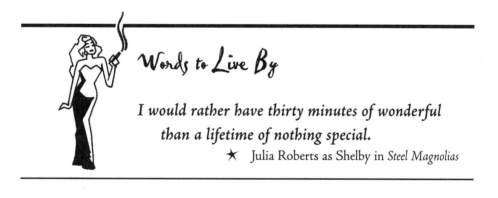

Words to Live By

I would rather have thirty minutes of wonderful than a lifetime of nothing special.
★ Julia Roberts as Shelby in *Steel Magnolias*

■ *Tender Mercies* (1983)
Stars: Robert Duvall, Tess Harper, Betty Buckley
Director: Bruce Beresford
Writer: Horton Foote

Tender Mercies is about the small blessings that can make loss more endurable, and about the very real heartaches that lie beneath an overwrought country music ballad.

Mac (Robert Duvall), a washed-up, drunken ex–country music singer/composer, stumbles into the backyard of a roadside motel, throws a temper tantrum at a garbage can lid, and passes out. The hotel is owned by Rosa Lee (Tess Harper), a young widow, and her preteen son, Sonny (Allan Hubbard). Rosa Lee gives the drifter a room, and when he has no money to pay his bill, puts him to work in the yard, insisting only that he not drink while he is working there. Eventually they marry, and through Rosa Lee's tender loving care, Mac is able to rebuild his shattered life. But then he must face the casualties caused by his drinking, including his relationship with his daughter.

Watch this movie when you know you ought to count your blessings, even if you have to use a magnifying glass to do so. *Tender Mercies* reminds us that sometimes the smallest gifts are the most merciful.

Bev's Culinarytherapy: Food for Every Mood

Comfort Food

When you're feeling like roadkill on the highway of life, there's nothing like food designed purely for pleasure to make you feel better. Here are a few of our favorite comfort foods to help you feel nurtured and loved from the inside out.

Mom's Mashed Potato Pie

3 pounds potatoes	2 teaspoons lemon juice
butter	1 teaspoon nutmeg
milk	salt and pepper
1 pound ground beef	two pinches hot ground
1/2 pound ground pork	red pepper
1/2 pound ground veal	2 eggs, beaten
1 large onion, chopped	

. . . continued

Boil, peel, and mash the potatoes with a whole bunch of butter and milk, and if you're really feeling down, use cream. Brown the meat and onion. Add the lemon juice, nutmeg, salt, pepper, and red pepper to the meat. In a greased casserole dish, make one layer of mashed potatoes, then add the meat-and-onion mixture, and top with the rest of the mashed potatoes. Brush the top of the mashed potatoes with two beaten eggs and bake at 350° for 45 minutes. Let stand for 10 minutes, eat as much as you possibly can as quickly as you possibly can, then roll over and take a nap. You're going to need it.

Bitter-and-Blue Chocolate Fondue

1 tablespoon butter	30 large marshmallows
1 pound chocolate candy	$\frac{1}{2}$ cup milk
bars with nuts	$\frac{1}{2}$ pint heavy cream

Grease a slow cooker with butter and set on high for 10 minutes. Then break up the chocolate and throw it in the pot along with all of the other high-calorie ingredients. Cover and set on low and cook until everything is melted and mushed together. Stir it occasionally so nothing burns or sticks, then uncover and dip whatever you can think of into the fondue.

Some dipping suggestions: pound cake, donuts, pretzels, dried apricots, your finger, your friend's finger, etc.

■ *The Deep End of the Ocean* (1999)

Stars: Michelle Pfeiffer, Treat Williams, Whoopi Goldberg, John Kapelos, Ryan Merriman, Jonathan Jackson

Director: Ulu Grosbard

Writer: Stephen Schiff, based on the novel by Jacquelyn Mitchard

It's hard to imagine a loss bigger than Beth and Pat Cappadora's: their three-year-old son, Ben, was kidnapped when Beth (Michelle Pfeiffer) was distracted for a moment. Gone is their dear son, their illusions of control, their sense of permanence, their familiar family dynamic, and just about anything else Beth can think of when she isn't curled up in bed in a fetal position trying to escape to dreamland. But as is often the case with loss, it has a hidden gift: it helps us to grow by making us dig more deeply into ourselves and take stock. And the good news here is that even though you'll be sobbing into handfuls of tissues, just when you're ready to say, "Why am I putting myself through this?" the kid shows up. *Phew!*

But of course, just as in real life, the complications don't end when what is lost is found. Ben is now a preteen who is deeply bonded to George (John Kapelos), who is his father figure (we won't explain why, but he is actually a good guy), and he can't remember anything about his family. While the police investigator (Whoopi Goldberg), Beth, and even Ben's older brother, Vince (Jonathan Jackson), are beating themselves up with guilt over what they did or didn't do, and Pat (Treat Williams) is busy making birdhouses and pretending everything's just hunky-dory, Ben (Ryan Merriman) struggles to make sense of his conflicting emotions. Eventually the Cappadoras have to accept that when we dwell on what should have been, we can miss what is. And "what is" turns out not to be such a terrible thing after all.

Ready to admit that the difference between your past and present is less extreme than night and day? If you're in the mood for some closure, this movie will let you have a good cathartic cry about what you lost, then give you that push forward into the future that you know you need.

■ *Dead Calm* (1989)
Stars: Sam Neill, Nicole Kidman, Billy Zane
Director: Phillip Noyce
Writer: Terry Hayes, based on the novel by Charles Williams

In the first five minutes of this film, Rae Ingram (Nicole Kidman) and her husband, John (Sam Neill), suffer a loss far greater than most of us can imagine, a loss they hope to heal by sailing their boat into idyllic and warm blue waters twelve hundred miles from land. Unfortunately, they decide to play Good Samaritan to Hughie Warriner (Billy Zane), a twitchy young man with a dubious story about why he abandoned his own ship. Before you know it, John and Rae are each battling separately for survival, John in an abandoned and sinking boat and Rae in the clutches of a lunatic bogeyman. As they race against time, Rae discovers that despite her recent devastating loss, her will to live is present after all. And before she loses yet another person she loves, she'll go down kicking, screaming, punching, poisoning, and psychologically manipulating. Now if only she could just get to that damned shotgun and splatter his guts all over the deck in a climactic and visceral scene that would exorcise all her demons. And if only the director would have restrained himself and given us a few less shots of Nicole Kidman's derriere for the guys and a few more of her looking grimly determined for us gals. Who knew Nicole could kick serious butt?

Angry about your recent loss? Feeling furious at the unfairness of it all? Watch this adrenaline-pumping thriller about a couple whose loss brings them together instead of pulling them apart, and enjoy seeing justice prevail, at least for tonight.

Can I Speak to a Supervisor?

Lower your shields and surrender your ships. We will add your biological and technological distinctiveness to our own. Your culture will adapt to serve us. Resistance is futile. We are the Borg.

★ "The Borg" in *Star Trek: First Contact*

Chapter 10

Ancient Chinese Secret, Huh?: Searching for Greater Meaning Movies

Whether it's the Bible or the Bhagavad Gita, acupuncture or the Atkins Diet, anarchy or the almighty dollar, we all need something to believe in. When we're at one of those bleak and unforgiving stretches of our inner highway, and there's no road sign or rest stop in sight, the big questions can really start to trouble us. Like, where is the next damn exit? What is the meaning of it all? Why am I here? Is there an afterlife? And is it really a good idea to carb deplete on a long-term basis?

If you have dotted all your *i*'s and crossed all your *t*'s but the sentence of your life still doesn't make sense, then watch one of these Searching for Greater Meaning Movies about people who come face-to-face with the spiritual subtext of the universe, and feed your soul.

■ *Chocolat* (2000)

Stars: Juliette Binoche, Johnny Depp, Lena Olin, Judi Dench, Alfred Molina
Director: Lasse Hallström
Writer: Robert Nelson Jacobs, based on the novel by Joanne Harris

If you're feeling like the Mardi Gras of life has passed you by, throw a Fat Tuesday feast for yourself with *Chocolat*, a movie that carries you to a magical land where the right piece of candy can cure anything from a fractured mother/daughter relationship to a fear of intimacy.

Vianne Rocher (Juliette Binoche) blows in with the north wind, unsettling the sedate life of an anachronistic French village by opening up a mystical, Mayan-inspired *chocolaterie* during Lent. The mayor of the town, Le Comte de Reynaud (Alfred Molina), knows that Vianne's melt-away truffles are a threat to his low-calorie control of the town and does his sugar-busting best to shut the shop down, but the sweet tooth of the villagers has been awakened and is hungry for more. What results is a battle between sweet and sour, paganism and monotheism, indulgence and abstinence. We'll let you guess which one wins out when there's that much homemade fudge around!

Chocolat proves that chocolate really is a metaphor for life. Sometimes it's butter cream, sometimes it's bittersweet, and sometimes it's Johnny Depp on a riverboat. Watch this one when you're feeling sour and deprived and see if it doesn't reawaken your sweet tooth for the high-caloric richness of experience.

■ *Life Is Beautiful* (1998)

Stars: Roberto Benigni, Nicoletta Braschi, Giorgio Cantarini
Director: Roberto Benigni
Writers: Vincenzo Cerami, Roberto Benigni

There are some people for whom the glass isn't just half-full, but practically brimming over with the sweetest nectar of the gods. These are the type of people we like to spend time with whenever we're in a deep funk and feeling pessimistic about it all. And they're definitely people we want by our side whenever fascist forces are in the neighborhood.

Guido Orefice (Roberto Benigni) is one of those rare people. He woos a woman named

Dora (Nicoletta Braschi) with his magical approach to life. Then, years later, as the Nazis close in on him, his wife, Dora, and his little boy, Giosué (Giorgio Cantarini), Guido paints the world with positive strokes of positivity, joy, and humor. Even when the family is sent to a concentration camp, Guido manages to convince his son that they're all just playing a big game (grand prize: a tank), shielding him from the evil and horror in the camp.

All right, it's a totally absurd concept, but trust us, when you're actually watching the movie, it works. Roberto Benigni is delightful as the playful fellow who refuses to give in to self-pity or sorrow, and who believes in the power of the mind to effect change in his world. And while we know that little Giosué is someday going to learn the truth of what was happening all around him, when you're feeling that there's just no positive way to spin the events of your life, *Life Is Beautiful* is sure to spark at least a little optimism inside of you. Moreover, it can help you to understand that even the most grim reality can be transformed through the power of a positive perspective.

Nancy's Momentous Minutiae: Sacrificing for the Cause

Tom Hanks donated his salary for *Forrest Gump* (1994) to the underpaid and underappreciated screenwriter.

Cary Grant donated his salary for *The Philadelphia Story* (1940) to the British war effort and his salary for *Arsenic and Old Lace* (1944) to the American war effort.

Joan Crawford, cast in *They All Kissed the Bride* (1942) after the leading lady, Carole Lombard, was killed in a plane crash while selling war bonds, donated her salary to the war effort. And when she discovered her agent had taken his usual 10 percent cut, she canned him.

■ *Mesmer* (1994)
   Stars: Alan Rickman, Amanda Ooms
   Director: Roger Spottiswoode
   Writer: Dennis Potter

While today we think of Western medicine as a rational and objective science (or at least, it is until you get managed care involved), this biopic of the controversial eighteenth-century psychiatrist Franz Anton Mesmer, who invented mesmerization, shows us that Western medicine has its roots in spiritual healing, and that faith is one of the most important weapons in the fight against suffering.

Franz Mesmer (Alan Rickman) attends a concert given by Maria Paradies (Amanda Ooms), a young, blind, and beautiful prodigy who is afflicted with bouts of mental illness that have mystified medical science. During the concert Maria has a fit, and Mesmer manages to "heal" her pain using his highly controversial and revolutionary theories of animal magnetism. Maria, who much prefers Mesmer's method of sensual healing to the head braces, eye screws, and leeches that her physicians employ, demands that her father send her to Mesmer on a regular basis. Doctor and patient begin a treatment/love affair as Mesmer attempts to calm Maria's fits and open her eyes to a kinder and more loving world.

Mesmer is an exploration of the world of faith and its role in physical and psychological well-being, and the thin line that often exists between charlatanism and genius and seeing God and having an orgasm. Watch this one when you need a reminder that when it comes to healing the uncharted regions of the human spirit, sometimes what matters is not the meat, but the motion.

■ *Oh, God!* (1977)
   Stars: John Denver, George Burns, Teri Garr
   Director: Carl Reiner
   Writer: Larry Gelbart

Imagine a dialogue with the Divine that sounds like sketch comedy from the golden era of television. Imagine God looks like George Burns in horn-rimmed glasses and a fishing cap. Now imagine John Denver as a prophet. Yes, we're still trying to get that frightening image out of our brains decades later.

But of course, in true Judeo-Christian tradition, God has a knack for picking on some poor schmuck and assigning him some huge undertaking, like gathering two of each species and building an ark to hold them, or expecting an assistant manager of Food World in Burbank to spread the gospel of kindness and love to the masses. This time God's messenger is the meek and stuttering Jerry Landers (John Denver in all his wire-rimmed-glasses, blond-bowl-cut, wide-belt-and-tight-hip-hugger seventies glory). Jerry is understandably skeptical at first, as is his wife, Bobbie (Teri Garr). But a couple of minor miracles later, Jerry's more than willing to believe and to tell people to stop being mean to each other (God's teachings here aren't exactly Kierkegaardesque). Eventually Jerry's enthusiastic and forthright declarations land him before a judge (in a scene shamelessly stolen from *Miracle on 34th Street*) and, as usual, God has to save the day.

Amid all the fast-paced Carl Reiner–type jokes about the nature of God, man, and miracles are some nuggets of wisdom that make this movie resonate like the sweetest of bell choirs. So if you're feeling a little distant from your spiritual self of late, watch *Oh, God!* and enjoy a lighthearted reminder that the sacred isn't so far away after all.

Stupid Girl Quotes

I don't see plays, 'cause I can nap at home for free. And I don't see movies 'cause they're trash, and they ain't got nothin' but naked people in 'em! And I don't read books, 'cause if they're any good they're gonna make 'em into a mini-series.

★ Shirley MacLaine as Ouiser in *Steel Magnolias*

■ *The Big Kahuna* (1999)
  Stars: *Kevin Spacey, Danny DeVito, Peter Facinelli*
  Director: *John Swanbeck*
  Writer: *Roger Rueff*

The Big Kahuna casts the desperate and high-pressure lives of industrial lubricant salesmen as a metaphor for the futility of all human endeavor, and the deep need that we all have to believe in something that is larger than ourselves.

Larry Mann (Kevin Spacey), a shining star salesman in the industrial lubricant business, and his partner, Phil Cooper (Danny DeVito), strategically arrange the hospitality suite at a manufacturers' convention to entertain potential customers. As they do so, they talk excitedly about what they are going to do when the Big Kahuna finally arrives, and they make that comeback swing for the bleachers, knocking out a huge sale and many commercial endorsements for the home team. A young trainee, Bob Walker (Peter Facinelli), works beside them, trying to learn the sales wisdom of the ages at their feet, and reconcile it with his own fundamentalist Christian beliefs. When the Big Kahuna chooses to materialize only to young Bob (probably because he's a card-carrying member of the God Squad), the two seasoned warhorses must lie back and wait for the rookie to deliver their salvation.

Watch this movie when your figures are down, and remember that some things aren't for sale, that Big Kahunas don't generally wear name tags, and that sometimes, despite a lifetime of experience and the best of intentions, we just have to let go and let Bob.

■ *The Filth and the Fury* (2000)
  Stars: *John Lydon, Paul Cook, Steve Jones, Glen Matlock,*
    Malcolm McClaren, Nancy Spungen, Sid Vicious
  Director: *Julien Temple*

This documentary of the seminal seventies punk band the Sex Pistols is about what happens when there's a garbage strike in Camelot, and a whole generation discovers simultaneously that the gods of queen, country, and proper sanitation have clay feet.

This film tracks the history of this legendary punk band, which for twenty-four epic months screamed to the world at large that the emperor had no clothes. And the world heard them, and has been hearing them ever since. Told largely through the eyes of Johnny Rotten and his doomed bassist, Sid Vicious, this movie offers a portrait of London in the seventies, when unemployment was soaring, the social structure disintegrating, and Kings Road was filled with revelers in bell-bottomed trousers and platform shoes, doing free interpretive dance on the deck of the *Titanic*.

Johnny Rotten and the Sex Pistols fired verbal volleys at the escapism that ignored the literal and figurative trash that was piling up ten feet high in London streets. From queen and country, to record companies and music managers, the Sex Pistols spit in the face of all authority.

When conditions become intolerable in your social system, and you suspect that a few of your household gods might have clay feet, court a little anarchy with the Sex Pistols, and rock the boat.

Nihilist Nuggets

I don't have any heroes. All useless. There's no heroes. None are accessible.

★ John Lydon, *The Filth and the Fury*

■ *Forrest Gump* (1994)
Stars: Tom Hanks, Robin Wright, Gary Sinise, Sally Field
Director: Robert Zemeckis
Writer: Eric Roth, based on the novel by Winston Groom

"Life is like a box of chocolates—you never know whatcha gonna get." But we think you know exactly what you're gonna get with a movie-of-the-year Oscar-winner featuring the ever-amiable Tom Hanks: smooth-as-caramel humor, sweet-as-chocolate philosophy, and a bittersweet ending that will have your eyes welling up with tears. Oh, we could quibble about the shaky chronology of the story (how could they have forgotten that the smiley face predated the running craze by several years?), and we could pick apart the absurdity of Forrest telling his entire life story while waiting for a bus (how slow *is* the public transportation in this town?). And we could play PC police and demand that Forrest's girlfriend, Jenny (Robin Wright), be granted just a moment in her adult life when she's not the ultimate weak female victim. Seriously, the woman lived through the 1970s—didn't she happen across a consciousness-raising group at some point? If she could find an abusive boyfriend on every corner, couldn't she find a copy of *Ms.* magazine on a newsstand somewhere? And if Forrest could inspire Elvis to swing his pelvis and Lennon to imagine, couldn't he inspire Jenny to find a spark of self-esteem?

But in a world filled with not-so-random acts of selfishness and greed, it's nice to take a two-hour escape into an alternate reality where people are touched by a brief encounter with a character who has the heart and faith of a child. When you're feeling worn out from suffering the casual brutality of everyday life, pop in *Forrest Gump* and slip into an endorphin-fueled euphoria. It may be a fool's paradise, but it feels pretty good.

■ *Brother Sun Sister Moon* (1973)

Stars: Graham Faulkner, Judi Bowker, Leigh Lawson, Alec Guinness
Director: Franco Zeffirelli
Writers: Suso Checchi d'Amico, Kenneth Ross, Lina Wertmüller,
    Franco Zeffirelli

Brother Sun Sister Moon uses the Roman countryside, a Donovan soundtrack, and a Saint Francis of Assisi who looks like the newest addition to a boy band to remind us all about the beauty of simplicity.

This seventies-influenced adaptation of the life of Saint Francis casts Francis (Graham Faulkner) as a flower child of the Dark Ages who awakens from a lengthy coma following an injury sustained during the Crusades to discover that his near-death experience has changed him into a priest of love. He drops out and turns on to a simpler life lived closer to God. Francis eschews his father's wealth, casts off the embroidered tunics and silk hosiery of the time, dons a flowing white caftan like you used to see in head shops on the

Haight, and takes up residence in a ruined church outside of town, determined to live like the birds and lilies of the field. Then, one by one, the other scions of the town's founding fathers cast their lot in with Francis, who seems to have found the secret to happiness outside the world of privilege and ill-gotten gains.

This is a great movie to watch when you're having a tough time making ends meet, and everything, including inspiration, is in short supply. The story of Saint Francis, like *It's a Wonderful Life*, reminds us all that the richest man in town is the one who is richest in love.

Jesus Christ Movie Star

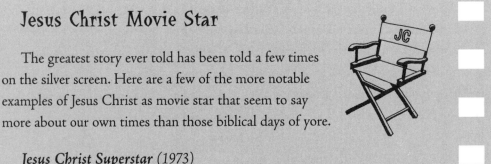

The greatest story ever told has been told a few times on the silver screen. Here are a few of the more notable examples of Jesus Christ as movie star that seem to say more about our own times than those biblical days of yore.

Jesus Christ Superstar (1973)
Stars: Ted Neeley, Carl Anderson, Yvonne Elliman
Director: Norman Jewison
*Writers: Melvyn Bragg, Norman Jewison, based on the play by Andrew
    Lloyd Weber and Tim Rice*

This version of the passion play casts JC as a sixties-style love child in long hair and sandals who belts out his gospel like a rock anthem, hangs around with beggars and prostitutes in his down time, takes on the oppression inherent in the system, and ultimately ascends to rock god heaven after an early and tragic death at the hands of a corrupt establishment. Watch this one when you need to feel that God is not only on your side, but is probably a very viable choice as a headliner at your next rock relief global simulcast.

. . . *continued*

Godspell *(1973)*
Stars: Victor Garber, David Haskell
Director: David Greene
Writers: David Greene, John-Michael Tebelak

A seventies camp classic, *Godspell* presents a warm and fuzzy—and decidedly nonthreatening and asexual—Jesus, who wears rainbow suspenders, a Superman T-shirt, painted tears, and a white-boy-afro wig. The updated JC is paternalistic and moody as he tells parables in King Jamesian English to a bright-eyed group of hippies who dance and face-paint their way to enlightenment while belting out rock ballads like "When Wilt Thou Save the People" in a manner frighteningly reminiscent of those stagy kids on *Barney and Friends* or one of those embarrassing acting exercises designed to free performers from inhibitions that they should probably hold on to. Watch this when you're in the mood for a kinder, gentler Judeo-Christian patriarch who shows mercy to those who practice bad theater improv and reminds us all that if you want to get to heaven, all you have to do is embrace your inner clown. Honk Honk.

The Last Temptation of Christ *(1988)*
Stars: Willem Dafoe, Harvey Keitel, Barbara Hershey
Director: Martin Scorsese
Writer: Paul Schrader, based on the novel by Nikos Kazantzakis

This is the urban, gritty eighties-style interpretation of the passion play as only Scorsese can tell it, with lots of atmospheric slow-mo dolly shots, the clipped bare bones dialogue of the street, an atmospheric soundtrack, a Judas from Delancey Street (Harvey Keitel), and a fiercely human Jesus Christ (Willem Dafoe), who must overcome a guilty conscience and moral confusion to complete his mission here on earth. Watch this when you need to remember that even our most celebrated archetypal heroes have to wrestle with the dark side.

. . . continued

Jesus of Montreal (1989)
Stars: Lothaire Bluteau, Catherine Wilkening
Director and Writer: Denys Arcand

Christianity and the Stanislavsky system meet in this Canadian film about a group of actors who are hired by their local parish to update and perform the passion play. When the actors begin internalizing their roles, and reinterpreting the Gospel with a decidedly radical bent, their method performances begin to rattle the powers that be as they head toward a crucifixion of a whole different color. Watch this when you need to remember that sometimes being Christlike means not being afraid to wreck the temple.

Words to Live By

I suppose I could be pissed off about what happened to me. But it's hard to stay mad when there's so much beauty in the world. Sometimes I feel like I'm seeing it all at once, and it's too much. My heart fills up like a balloon that's about to burst.

★ Kevin Spacey as Lester Burnham in *American Beauty*

■ *The Sixth Sense* (1999)
Stars: Bruce Willis, Haley Joel Osment, Toni Collette
Director and Writer: M. Night Shyamalan

To make the most of our gifts, *The Sixth Sense* tells us, we must embrace our fears. Hey, it's a wonderfully enriching philosophy, but it's kind of hard for eight-year-old Cole Sear

(Haley Joel Osment) to appreciate when all day long he sees dead people screeching at him as they walk around with hatchets buried in their heads and faces blown off. No wonder the kid's a prime candidate for antianxiety medication.

Dr. Malcolm Crowe (Bruce Willis) is the child psychologist determined to get to the bottom of Cole's secret terror. For Crowe, this one's personal: he'd barely had a chance to get fingerprints on the mirrored surface of the plaque announcing that he was child shrink of the year before he was confronted by a shivering and psychotic ex-patient (Donnie Wahlberg) he'd failed miserably years before. So while Cole has to learn a Jungian lesson about facing the darkness, and his mom (Toni Collette) has to learn patience as her preadolescent son struggles to tell her about his deepest secrets, Crowe has to learn to let go of his ego and his preconceived notions about dead people (clearly, he ought to have spent less time at the office and more time watching John Edward).

It's easy to miss all this Eastern philosophy and psychological theory in *The Sixth Sense* because it's such a compelling thriller with the kind of thoughtful direction that makes you want to watch it again the next night to figure out how you missed the obvious. Which brings us to our favorite lesson of this film: always pay attention to the details and the subtext unless you want to find yourself in a reality totally different from the one you thought you were in.

If you know you've been avoiding facing up to your fears of late, or you've been hiding your head in the sand of workaholism and ego gratification, check out *The Sixth Sense*. It will reassure you that when you face your fears, you'll find the universe is, ultimately, a benign place—and the only thing to fear is fear itself.

▪ ***Priest*** (1994)
  Stars: Linus Roache, Tom Wilkinson, Cathy Tyson
  Director: Antonia Bird
  Writer: Jimmy McGovern

In this ode to the redemptive power of forgiveness, the new junior priest in a small, working-class, Liverpool parish, Father Greg (Linus Roache), is appalled to discover that the senior priest he has been assigned to work with must've crossed his fingers behind his back when he took his chastity vow. Worse, Father Matthew (Tom Wilkinson) didn't just give in to overwhelming lust once and immediately repent—he's actually parked his mistress (Cathy Tyson) in the priests' common cottage and is carrying on a pseudomarriage. But while Father Greg angrily delivers a biblically based lecture to Father Matthew about defiance of God's law, he forgets that part about he who casts the first stone. Yep, before you know it the police blotter in the local paper is running a report on what Father Greg was caught doing one night after bar time—and it wasn't exactly polishing the communion chalice.

What ensues is a painful lesson for all in forgiveness, acceptance, and human frailty as the community, the priests, and the church hierarchy all wrestle with what to do about Father Greg. In the end, of course, it takes a child to lead them.

You could argue that *Priest* raises more questions than it answers, but when you've been nursing a grudge for far too long, watch this provocative movie and see if its lesson about the transformative power of forgiveness doesn't seem airtight to you.

Artificial Sweeteners

When you're desperately in need of a jolt of spirituality and willing to overlook shameless oversentimentality, you might find one of these artificially colored and sweetened feel-good flicks to your liking. Just don't blame us if you start feeling sluggish a half hour later.

Pay It Forward (2000)
Stars: Kevin Spacey, Helen Hunt, Haley Joel Osment
Director: Mimi Leder
Writer: Leslie Dixon, based on the novel by Catherine Ryan Hyde

Assigned by his seventh-grade social studies teacher Eugene Simonet (Kevin Spacey) to make the world a better place, tender-eyed little Trevor McKinney (Haley Joel Osment) comes up with an improvement on random

. . . continued

acts of kindness—he's going to do good deeds for three people and tell them to "pay it forward" to three more people . . . and so on, and so on. Eventually the world should end up not with a gazillion lines of e-mail addresses before you hit the meat of the message, but with positive energy overflowing and transforming it into a better place. Of course, the Pay It Forward movement will end up in Los Angeles, where it will become the hottest trend and spawn coverage on the nightly news, a simple stick figure graphic that looks great on a movie marquee, and widespread rejection of pessimism and defeatism.

Hey, we were into the romance between the wounded and troubled Arlene (Helen Hunt) and the nebbishy and badly disfigured Eugene, and we wanted to scoop up that darling little Haley Joel into our arms and give him a bear hug. But it's hard to give in to that millennium-hugging, white-light-visualizing, decidedly noncynical feeling when this movie insists on sending its message into your mind with the force of a two-by-four striking your head. By the time the candlelight vigil came along, we were downright cranky.

Still, if you're sorely in need of an uplift, and willing to make a concerted effort to squelch your brain functioning and give in to the schmaltz, you might want to check this one out.

Patch Adams (1998)
Stars: Robin Williams, Monica Potter, Philip Seymour Hoffman, Bob Gunton, Daniel London
Director: Tom Shadyac
Writer: Steve Oedekerk, based on the book Gesundheit: Good Health Is a Laughing Matter *by Hunter "Patch" Adams and Maureen Mylander*

Speaking of squelching your brain functioning, this is another one of those movies that demand you turn off your mind and float downstream, but at least it doesn't require a full-frontal lobotomy. It does, however, require a high tolerance for overly cute kids, vaudeville humor, and cheap emotional

. . . *continued*

setups like the overwrought packed-balcony courtroom scene (totally ripped off from *To Kill a Mockingbird*).

Former mental patient Hunter "Patch" Adams (Robin Williams) has decided his life's purpose is to help people. Bright-eyed and bushy-tailed Patch, who seems to have an endless supply of hideously loud seventies shirts and anachronistic cargo pants, figures the best way to fulfill his life's mission is to enroll in medical school. Once there, Patch is such a quick study that he has plenty of time for high jinks—entertaining youthful cancer patients by donning a red rubber nose fashioned from an enema bulb, filling rooms with balloons, and helping a dying elderly woman to swim in a pool full of noodles.

But just as the gags are running a bit thin, the movie takes a somber turn and opens us up to questioning the power of love and joy in the face of evil. And when Patch reaches his lowest point in a mountain Gethsemane, the smallest of creatures teaches him his most important lesson—that while we cannot change every corner of the world we must do our best to change the corner we inhabit. It's this moment and a handful of quiet little truths sprinkled among the pratfalls that saves *Patch Adams* from being hopelessly corny as it encourages us to follow our dreams and find purpose in service to our fellow man.

If you've been feeling lost in the woods lately, *Patch Adams* may get you back on your personal path.

■ *Holy Smoke* (1999)
Stars: Kate Winslet, Harvey Keitel
Director: Jane Campion
Writers: Anna Campion, Jane Campion

Ruth Barron (Kate Winslet), an intelligent and beautiful young Australian woman, goes in search of deeper meaning in the heady back alleys of India, and winds up smitten with a spiritual leader called Baba, who opens her third eye and reveals to her the simple beauty and interconnectedness of all creation. In other words, Ruth gets blissed out big time, starts wearing brightly colored caftans, and chants and meditates a lot, which makes everybody from her former life really, really nervous. Meanwhile, her unenlightened family back in the Australian equivalent of the trailer park fears that they have lost their daughter forever. They hire world-renowned cult deprogrammer P. J. Waters (Harvey Keitel) to rescue Ruth from her nirvana.

Holy Smoke pits two able adversaries with opposing genders and beliefs in a struggle to the death. Isolated on a ranch in the middle of a distinctly Freudian Australian outback, masculine and feminine, reason and mysticism, sex and love, wrestle over the fundamental questions of the universe, like, what is the difference between faith and delusion, is control worth the cost, how do men really feel about the power of the goddess, and just what is Jane Campion's fascination with Harvey Keitel's naked body anyway?

Watch this movie when you're between the horns of a spiritual dilemma and need to be reminded that in a world where truth is relative, kindness is the only absolute.

Don't Be Afraid to Ask the Important Questions

Is life just a game where we make up the rules while we're searching for something to say? Or are we just simply spiraling coils of self-replicating DNA?

★ Eric Idle in *Monty Python's The Meaning of Life*

What if the hokeypokey really is what it's all about?

★ Anonymous

The Meaning of Life According to Monty Python

When it comes to figuring out the meaning of it all, we've always thought that the Monty Python crew was on to something. If you're in the mood for absurd, hypereducated, hilarious, and thought-provoking commentary on the important stuff, check out what John Cleese, Eric Idle, Michael Palin, and the rest of the gang have to say in these classic Python flicks.

The Life of Brian (1979)

This is an irreverent spin on the proliferation of mystery cults at the beginning of the Christian Era, starring Graham Chapman as the hapless Brian, born in the manger next door to you-know-who. *The Life of Brian* pokes fun at our human foibles: our cliquishness, our childish need for perfect leaders, and mostly, our desire to have someone else figure it all out and present it to us as a nonthreatening homily that allows us to remain in our comfort zone. Watch this when you are ready to laugh at your own failings, and remember, always look on the bright side of life. . . .

Monty Python and the Holy Grail (1975)

In this King Arthur spoof, various knights of the round table must prove themselves worthy of the grail they seek and answer the deeper questions, like "What is the airspeed velocity of an unladen swallow?" (Hey, knowing the answer to this one once got us out of having to flash picture IDs to get our bar bracelets at a concert.) As the knights travel across England, they encounter everything from shrubbery-demanding bandits to snotty French castle guards to a man-eating bunny.

When you feel yourself wandering in the backwaters of your own personal journey, *Monty Python and the Holy Grail* will keep you laughing and remind you that there's no escaping life's absurdities and perplexities.

. . . *continued*

Monty Python's The Meaning of Life (1983)

The most uneven of the Python movies, and easily the most tasteless one (it's hard to stomach the exploding glutton scene, and the *Oliver*-esque musical number about the Vatican position on birth control is either side-splittingly brilliant or horrifyingly offensive depending on your perspective), this movie nevertheless has nuggets of absolute genius. And yes, the Pythons do reveal the ultimate secret to the meaning of our very existence, but hey, we don't want to be spoilers.

■ *The Wizard of Oz* (1939)
Stars: *Judy Garland, Frank Morgan, Ray Bolger, Bert Lahr, Jack Haley, Billie Burke*
Director: *Victor Fleming, Richard Thorpe*
Writers: *Noel Langley, Florence Ryerson, Edgar Allan Woolf, based on the novel*
  The Wonderful Wizard of Oz *by L. Frank Baum*

Alright, we know you've seen this movie fourteen million times, but there's a reason you keep coming back to it, a reason every gift shop you've ever been in has a porcelain Glinda statue or a Toto pin, a reason it's national news every time they auction off those ruby slippers again: *The Wizard of Oz* speaks straight to our hearts. Dorothy Gale (Judy Garland, of course) is the lonely girl inside all of us who wants more than what her black-and-white world has to offer her, who takes an archetypal journey through colorful lands and dark woods, and who ultimately discovers that what she seeks is within. And like Dorothy's friends in Oz, we have all learned in our own way that the treasures we most dearly long for can't be bestowed upon us by some paternalistic outside force; rather, we must earn them ourselves by facing life's challenges. And haven't we all discovered the power of a to-die-for pair of red pumps?

Whatever your life crisis, *The Wizard of Oz* is the cinematic equivalent of s'mores. Indulge, savor the sweetness and the warmth, and pay no attention to that subtext about not leaving your own backyard and going adventuring.

Chapter 11

Pay No Attention to the Man Behind the Curtain: Control Issue Movies

Let's face it, the world is a chaotic and random place. No matter how carefully we plan, the normal twists and turns of fortune can leave us feeling a little powerless, like we're stalling out midair. We often find ourselves white-knuckling the joystick of life, or plunging ourselves into a tailspin, not enjoying the ride at all.

When you find yourself trying to defy gravity with the sheer lift and thrust of your willpower rather than trusting the forces of aerodynamics, hit the button on your ejector seat, watch one of these Control Issue Movies, and experience the bliss of free fall.

■ *Ordinary People* (1980)

Stars: Mary Tyler Moore, Donald Sutherland, Judd Hirsch,
  Timothy Hutton, Elizabeth McGovern
Director: Robert Redford
Writer: Alvin Sargent, based on the novel by Judith Guest

Ordinary People is a story about what happens when you try to control the things that you can't change while ignoring the things that you can, and about how many different emotions Mary Tyler Moore's character can suppress in the same movie without spontaneously combusting.

Mary Tyler Moore, our lovable Laura Petrie/Mary Richards, plays Beth, a WASP-ish, deeply conflicted modern-day Medea who is engaged in a methodical attempt to psychologically and emotionally murder her younger son because she can't accept the death of her eldest. What, we wonder, has happened to our accessible but elegant Jackie Kennedy of the suburbs? This just goes to show you what can happen to even the most mediagenic among us when we're in the throes of a control freak meltdown.

Meanwhile, back at the north shore ranch, her grief-stricken younger son, Conrad (Timothy Hutton), has a severe case of survivor's guilt. He even tries to commit suicide after the boating accident that spared him but killed his brother. But Beth, a devout follower of the "if we don't talk about it, it will go away" school of grief management, wants Conrad to just get over it already and quit mucking up perfectly good cocktail parties with his psychic agony. In the end, Beth discovers what we all discover when we try to avoid pain by denying reality: what you don't know can hurt you, and everyone else around you too.

Watch this one when you've got some difficult emotions of your own to face up to, and let *Ordinary People* remind you that the only way to heal is to allow yourself to feel.

■ *Cast Away* (2001)

Stars: Tom Hanks, Helen Hunt
Director: Robert Zemeckis
Writer: William Broyles, Jr.

"We live and die by the clock!" Chuck Noland (Tom Hanks) shouts at his crew of Soviet FedEx workers who haven't yet internalized the American obsession with efficiency.

Chuck, babe, rule number one: when you tempt fate, it comes back to bite you in the butt. Devoted to his job, Chuck once again puts aside the needs of his girlfriend, Kelly (Helen Hunt), and hops on an airplane at Christmas to resolve some snafu down in Malaysia, then wakes from a much-needed nap to discover that while he was out, the pilot was veering off course and losing radio contact. Next thing you know, the plane's in a nosedive, Chuck is trying to remember what all those stewardesses always said about where the inflatable flotation device is stored, and his world comes crashing down somewhere in the Pacific.

You know the rest—several hours of Tom Hanks trying to suck water out of coconuts, fashion a loincloth, and keep from going crazy by conversing with "Wilson," a volleyball on which he's painted a face. Chuck's transformation from a pudgy middle manager in a fisherman's sweater to a scrawny spearfisher with gray-blond rasta locks is as dramatic as his change from a workaholic who goes nowhere without his pager to a survivor who can spend two solid months fashioning rope from tree bark. (And can we just point out that whoever did Chuck's hair once he was rescued from that raft did an amazing job of not only shaping his do but restoring the rich brown color and luster to his locks?)

When you know you need to slow down, try carving out three hours of you-time and pop in *Cast Away.* It's a sobering lesson in what happens when we lose track of our priorities and become obsessed with taming time.

Get a Grip, Hon

Tye Graham (Michael Wilding): Did you ever hear of "defense mechanism"?
Jenny Stewart (Joan Crawford): You mean, a girdle?

★ from *Torch Song*

Hoopskirt Dreams, Part 2: The Black-and-White Years

Much as we love to live in the modern era of blue jeans and all-cotton sweatsuits (not to mention washing machines with delicate cycles, and home dry-cleaning kits), we can't help wishing that for just a moment we could return to the era of white gloves, smart suits, and silly hats. By watching these classic films, you too can vicariously enjoy being draped by Adrian, Orry-Kelly, and Edith Head.

Love on the Run (1936)

Joan Crawford runs away from her dreary life as a socialite, but despite being an ocean away from her funds and her closet (in the days before credit cards—what a horror!), she somehow ends up in an endless array of scrumptious outfits. She jumps into a stolen truck and discovers a darling white organdy gown complete with polka dot sequins and a matching hair ribbon, and she gets kidnapped by a man who inexplicably insists that she don a black velvet cloak with a bejeweled clip and mink cuffs. Would that our own wildcap adventures were so well costumed! And check out her ultrachic shades when she's incognito. *Gowns by Adrian.*

Theodora Goes Wild (1936)

If you're going to go wild, you might as well do it in style, as Irene Dunne does in this madcap comedy about a woman who lets her hair down. Set free from the polka-dot-sack-dress bunch back home in little old Lynnfield, Connecticut, Theodora spends her savings on one over-the-top ensemble after another. One day she's swimming in a white ostrich feather cape and

. . . continued

accenting it with chunky rhinestone jewelry and a plume on her head that bobs merrily as she chats with reporters at a press conference. The next day she's in a black gown with a down-to-there neckline that ends in a humongous white cloth calla lily. And of course, there's the requisite Depression-era symbol of dreams: the lamé gown with matching fur-trimmed cape. *Costumes by Bernard Newman.*

Mr. Skeffington (1944)

Bette Davis as Fanny may be petulant, shallow, and vain, but she looks so fab in her getups that you start to see why everyone puts up with all of her cold manipulations and abuse. We just love the black satin spaghetti strap gown with net shawl, huge flowers at the bust and waist, and dripping diamonds, and the beaded and fringed flapper dress with lamé cap and cigarette holder. But that shawl made out of dead foxes . . . somehow the luxury of consumption seems a bit too viscerally challenging when you've got animal heads hanging off you, no? And the stuffed-bird hat will leave you in fashion shock. *Gowns by Orry-Kelly.*

To Each His Own (1946)

As a 1920s businesswoman, Josephine "Jodie" Norris (Olivia de Havilland) parades about in a variety of smart suits and art deco hats, with plenty of fur and feathers and always-appropriate pearls. At night, she steps out in a gold lamé gown with a draping front and back and matching bolero with mink cuffs. Really, it's hard to believe that a woman willing to make the fashion choices in this movie hasn't got the gumption to stand up to small-town morality and demand her right to be respected as a single mom with impeccable taste. *Costumes by Edith Head.*

In a Perfect World . . .

Hate him?! How could I hate him? Mothers don't hate their sons! Is that what he told you? You see how you believe everything he tells you? And you can't do the same for me, you can't! God I don't know what anyone wants from me anymore!

★ Mary Tyler Moore as Beth in *Ordinary People*

But I'd like the pie heated, and I don't want the ice cream on top. I want it on the side, and I'd like strawberry instead of vanilla if you have it. If not, then no ice cream, just whipped cream, but only if it's real. If it's out of the can, then nothing.

★ Meg Ryan as Sally Albright in *When Harry Met Sally*

■ *The Out-of-Towners* (1970)
Stars: Jack Lemmon, Sandy Dennis
Director: Arthur Hiller
Writer: Neil Simon

The Out-of-Towners is a control queen's nightmare, which sacrifices two innocent tourists on the altar of mass transit and bad weather and strands them helpless at 3 A.M. in New York City.

George Kellerman (Jack Lemmon), a typical sixties-style type-A businessman with a good briefcase and a bad attitude, is scheduled to fly to New York City with his wife, Gwen (Sandy Dennis), for a job interview. Just to be on the safe side, George plans to arrive a day early and take in dinner and a show. But they encounter bad weather over Boston, and from that very first air pocket, this couple is hit with enough logistical turbulence to down a jumbo jet.

All of us control queens can learn a lot from this movie by focusing on the two diametrically opposed management styles employed by husband and wife. Gwen is willing to acknowledge that things aren't going according to plan and just go with the flow. George, on the other hand, keeps trying to kick ass and take names and . . . well, let's just put it this way: he never does make that important interview.

This is a great movie to watch when you're in the grip of something larger than yourself and need to remember that if you expect to survive a tidal wave, or a weekend in New York, sometimes it's best to roll with it.

👀 *So Nice They Made It Twice:* There was a remake starring Steve Martin and Goldie Hawn that has its charms, but we much prefer Jack Lemmon's iconic depiction of the American type-A personality adrift in a world spun beyond the bounds of his management techniques.

Facing Facts

Gwen Kellerman (Sandy Dennis): George, what are we going to do? We can't ride, we can't walk, we can't eat, and we can't pray.

George Kellerman (Jack Lemmon): Well, we can think. As long as we've got our brains, we can think.

Gwen Kellerman: Oh, they'll take that too, George. You'll see.

★ from *The Out-of-Towners*

▪ *Dancer in the Dark* (2000)
Stars: Björk, Catherine Deneuve, Peter Stormare, Vladica Kostic
Director and Writer: Lars von Trier

In this bizarre musical about the power of denial, which is in equal parts endearing and disturbing, Finnish singer/iconoclast, elfin-geek-girl, epitome-of-cool Björk plays Selma, a Czechoslovakian immigrant in Washington State in 1964 and the ultimate innocent. To support herself and her preteen son (Vladica Kostic), and to secretly save up for an expensive operation to prevent the boy from going blind, Selma works by day operating a punch press in a factory and by night assembling cards of bobby pins. Is it any wonder Selma daydreams incessantly about starring in a Hollywood musical? Preferably one that would show off her formidable tap-dancing talents as well as her singing, and one in which the stage would glow with the light of a thousand candles so that in her nearsightedness she won't fall off the stage into the orchestra pit.

Yes, Selma, like her son, is actually going blind, and it is becoming increasingly difficult to hide her failing vision. But rather than deal with her harsh reality, Selma uses the power of her imagination to transform the sounds of her world and the rhythms of her life into music that fuels her daydreams. It's an enormously effective defense mechanism, but as Selma comes to learn the hard way, that think-it-be-it attitude needs to be supplemented by practical actions—like, say, opening an account in a federally insured savings and loan instead of putting one's money in the nearest cookie tin. Selma stubbornly believes that her world will right itself without her changing her behavior, and ultimately her fantasy world becomes a destructive force.

If you're in the mood for a dose of reality served up in a hypersurrealistic way (imagine Björk spouting free-form lyrics as she waltzes with a bloodied murder victim), *Dancer in the Dark* will wake you up with its lesson: that just because we close our eyes doesn't mean our unpleasant realities go away, so relinquishing all control to fate is probably not a good idea.

Nancy's Momentous Minutiae: Acting on Instinct

During the filming of *Gone With the Wind*, Vivien Leigh and Olivia de Havilland were upset that woman-friendly director George Cukor had been replaced with action director Victor Fleming (who once, when Leigh asked his advice on how to play a scene, replied, "Ham it up"). Unbeknownst to each other, the actresses each secretly met with Cukor at his home to get his direction, and both wound up with Academy Award nominations for their performances.

■ *Strangers on a Train* (1951)

Stars: Robert Walker, Farley Granger, Ruth Roman, Patricia Hitchcock,
  Kasey Rogers
Director: Alfred Hitchcock
Writer: Raymond Chandler, Czenzi Ormonde, based on a novel by
  Patricia Highsmith, adapted by Whitfeld Cook

Hitchcock's ode to control freaks, this movie reminds us that we all have a dark side that we must keep in check lest chaos break loose—and that we ought to stay far, far away from middle-aged men who wear two-toned Oxfords and still live with Mom.

Farley Granger plays tennis star Guy Haines, who happily engages in friendly banter on the New York/D.C. train with a stranger named Bruno (Robert Walker), whose confrontational manner and choice of loud footwear ought to clue Guy in to the fact that Bruno is going to be more intrusive than your average busybody. Bruno suggests gamely that he and Guy swap murders—Bruno will do in Guy's ex-wife, Miriam (Kasey Rogers), and Guy will knock off Bruno's overbearing pop. Guy thinks nothing of this hypothetical nonsense and goes home, but once the unspeakable has been spoken, his world becomes as uncontrollable as John McEnroe in a rage. In scene after scene we're confronted with yet another example of what happens when we don't keep our tummies tucked in and our base emotions in check—a dead body, blackmail, and shockingly bad painting in a German postwar style.

As Guy tries desperately to contain Bruno's madness and keep the cops off his trail, things just spin further out of control until finally order is restored and justice is served. Really, this is the perfect movie to watch when you're feeling just a touch homicidal and in need of a dark little giggle. It'll remind you that sometimes a little repression of primal instincts can be a good thing.

Stupid Guy Quotes

How do you do, sir? I, uh, I'd like to talk with you sometime, sir, and tell you about my idea for harnessing the life force. It'll make atomic power look like a horse and buggy. I'm already developing my faculty for seeing millions of miles. And Senator, can you imagine being able to smell a flower . . . on the planet Mars? I'd like to, uh, have lunch with you someday soon, sir, and tell you more about it.

★ Robert Walker as Bruno Anthony in
Strangers on a Train

■ *Mary, Queen of Scots* (1971)
   Stars: *Vanessa Redgrave, Glenda Jackson, Timothy Dalton*
   Director: *Charles Jarrott*
   Writer: *John Hale*

In all of history, there has never been a greater control queen than England's Elizabeth I. This micromanager did not remain absolute ruler of her realm for more than forty years by letting go and letting God. Elizabeth kept her hands on the keys to the kingdom at all times, and nowhere is her historic skill for manipulation better staged than in *Mary, Queen of Scots*.

Widowed and orphaned on the same day, Mary (Vanessa Redgrave) leaves France and returns to Scotland to rule her homeland in her mother's stead, but her eye is set on the ultimate goal of recapturing the English throne for the Catholic church. Unfortunately, they aren't too crazy about Catholics in Mother England, so Queen Elizabeth (Glenda Jackson) adopts a scorched-earth policy toward both Catholicism and her sister's court. The intricacy of the emotional engineering that ensues will delight control connoisseurs everywhere as the virgin queen, like an Elizabethan James Bond, outmaneuvers the greatest military and political minds of her day, because she is able to put her head above her heart and make the tough calls.

Reel to Real

Queen Elizabeth I was crowned in 1558, when she was just twenty-five years old, and ruled England until her death in 1603. Elizabeth's cool head, firm hand, and crossed legs helped her to stabilize a politically volatile nation, and the last forty years of her reign are known as the "Golden Age."

Quips from Control Queens

Though God hath raised me high, yet this I count the glory of my crown: that I have reigned with your loves. And though you have had, and may have, many mightier and wiser princes sitting in this seat; yet you never had, nor shall have any that will love you better.

★ Elizabeth I

▪ *Sorry, Wrong Number* (1948)

Stars: Barbara Stanwyck, Burt Lancaster
Director: Anatole Litvak
Writer: Lucille Fletcher, based on her radio play

Leona Stevenson (Barbara Stanwyck) may be an invalid with a heart condition, but she knows what she wants out of life and isn't afraid to go for it. What a gal! Would that we all looked so poised and in control when bedridden—a lovely lace bed jacket, a clingy negligee that hugs a perfect figure, and a flawless coif. Sheesh, the woman hasn't been vertical in years—you'd think she'd at least suffer from bed head!

But all is not as it seems. Leona's steely will turns out to be less a shining example of her personal strength that we should emulate than a deep flaw in her character that's turned her into a hypochondriacal shrew. Hubby (Burt Lancaster) and Daddy cater to her every whim. But when Leona overhears a murder plot on the phone, she starts to realize that at least one person in her circle is beginning to revolt . . . and that her need for total control may have deadly consequences.

Sorry, Wrong Number offers a powerful lesson in the paradoxical reality that the more we try to control the more out of control we become. Hey, maybe unruly cowlicks aren't such a bad thing after all.

Pearls of Passive Aggression

Darlene (Robin Wright): Are you aware that you're yelling?
Eddie (Sean Penn): My voice is raised in emphasis. It's a perfectly legitimate use of volume.

★ from *Hurlyburly*

■ *Madame X* (1966)
Stars: Lana Turner, John Forsythe, Burgess Meredith,
Constance Bennett, Keir Dullea, Ricardo Montalban
Director: David Lowell Rich
Writer: Jean Holloway

At first it seems Holly Anderson (Lana Turner) has finally got it made. No longer stuck on the off-the-rack side of town, she has made it to the fashion big leagues by marrying a career diplomat (John Forsythe) who can keep her in plenty of John Louis gowns, David Webb jewels, and Ben Kahn furs. But then there's that scheming mother-in-law . . .

Okay, so Holly's been a little bored, and naive enough to start spending a lot of time out with the local womanizer (Ricardo Montalban), but she's a good girl, really. But then a horrible accident threatens to ruin Holly's reputation and bring her husband and son tumbling down with her. Ah! The mean old mother-in-law (Constance Bennett) finally has Holly caught in a web. Holly's choice: tell the truth, hope for the best, and risk destroying the lavish lifestyle of her loved ones and the glamorous career of her husband, or disappear and spare them the "pain" of embarrassment.

Now, we know what you're thinking—what about the pain of losing a wife and mother? Can't we give her family just a little credit for having their priorities straight? Well, we could, but then we wouldn't have the delight of watching Lana's wintry-blond hair go from petrified bubble to disheveled rag as she spirals into the depths of hell as an absinthe addict in Mexico sharing a room with Burgess Meredith. Will she put her pride aside and seize her last chance to reconnect with her son (Keir Dullea) and husband? Or will she wallow in martyrdom and despair until she comes to an unsavory end?

When you're in the mood for a stylish reminder that yachts, Connecticut estates, and blue-blood pedigrees are no match for honest communication with those you love—and that love means letting go of one's need to write all the scripts for those around us—watch *Madame X*.

👀 *So Nice They Made It Twice:* If you can locate a copy of the 1937 version with Gladys George, you're in for a real weepfest, especially in the courtroom scenes, which drip with irony.

Quips from Control Queens

Michele (Lisa Kudrow): Did you lose weight?
Romy (Mira Sorvino): Actually, I have been trying this new fat-free diet I invented. All I've had to eat for the past six days are gummy bears, jelly beans, and candy corns.

Michele: God, I wish I had your discipline.

★ from *Romy and Michele's High School Reunion*

■ *Serial Mom* (1994)
Stars: Kathleen Turner, Sam Waterston, Ricki Lake, Matthew Lillard
Director and Writer: John Waters

We've all had loved ones who are just a bit nudgey, but reworking our vacation plans or extracting ourselves from a pickle Mom created is nothing compared to what Beverly Sutphin's kids (Ricki Lake and Matthew Lillard) and husband (Sam Waterston) have to deal with. Beverly (Kathleen Turner) thinks she's just being a concerned, loving, and protective matriarch when she takes a fireplace poker to the boy who has just rejected her teen daughter, or uses her station wagon to mow down the teacher who unfairly graded her son's math test.

The blood-and-guts, gross-out humor in this black comedy definitely isn't for everyone, but even as you're disgusted by Waters's twisted vision of the overbearing surburban mom, you can't help noticing that there's a germ of truth beneath it all. Beverly's not the only one who feels compelled to control her seemingly perfect environment, or to lash out at those who hurt her kids rather than let them learn from their own painful experiences. She's just a little more extreme than most, which accounts for the blood smeared on the bottom of her pristine white Keds sneakers and the trail of death that stretches across the neighborhood.

So if you find yourself plotting absurd revenge scenarios or obsessing about someone else's problems, watch *Serial Mom* and have a laugh at the garish ugliness that lies beneath the carefully polished veneer of suburban America.

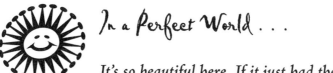 *In a Perfect World . . .*

It's so beautiful here. If it just had the New York Times, *it would be perfect.*
★　Janeane Garofalo as Marcy Tizard in *The Matchmaker*

See the way the handle on her pruning shears matches her gardening clogs? That's not an accident.
★　Kevin Spacey as Lester Burnham in *American Beauty*

Chapter 12

And Justice Will Prevail: Reassurance Movies

We know—we've been there too. You find yourself in circumstances beyond your control or even your understanding: no one seems to hear or believe you, much less cherish you and your unique gifts. You meant to be on the mountaintop, admiring the wildflowers and gazing out at the horizon, but somehow you ended up in the industrial valley, squinting through a layer of smog and wondering where you took a wrong turn.

If you're in the Gary, Indiana, of your life and longing fondly for a little ozone, watch one of these Reassurance Movies featuring folks who find themselves in grim circumstances but who, through their own perseverance, end up in a meadow of contentment, admiring the sunrise of new possibilities and justice for all. These cinematic equivalents of a shot of oxygen are just the thing to make you breathe easily again and to reassure you that no matter how dire your circumstances, every little thing will be alright in the end.

■ *The Shawshank Redemption* (1994)

Stars: Tim Robbins, Morgan Freeman
Director: Frank Darabont
Writers: Stephen King, Frank Darabont, based on the short story
  "Rita Hayworth and the Shawshank Redemption," by Stephen King

Okay, so it's a little weird to cast a story about the brutality and hopelessness of prison life as a Reassurance Movie. *The Shawshank Redemption*, however, is that rare film that manages to remind us that every dark cloud has a silver lining without denying the probability of rain. It also tells us that if you're willing to wait long enough, all wrongs will be righted, and the sun of justice and right reason will rise again.

Andy Dufresne (Tim Robbins) is a former bank executive who is wrongly imprisoned for the murder of his wife and her lover. Andy is sentenced to life without parole, and reconciles himself to the cruel realities of the world within the grim stone walls of Shawshank prison. He goes about his activities quietly, and even takes a job cooking the books for the warden, which allows him the freedom to make some positive changes, like the addition of a prison library. No matter how impossible his circumstances, Andy manages to "wade through a river of shit and come out clean" because he keeps his hopes pinned on the impossible dream of freedom.

Andy's remarkable story is narrated by Red Redding (Morgan Freeman), a sadder but wiser convict, who has a different philosophy about how to endure life without parole. Red has abandoned all hope, and spends his days trying to forget about the fact that there are places in the world that are not made out of cold stone and cruelty. For Red, the only freedom lies in complete surrender.

Of course, in the end, hope wins out over hopelessness, inspiration defeats resignation, and we are all left with that warm fuzzy feeling. *The Shawshank Redemption* reminds us that no matter the duration or severity of our wrongful imprisonment, if we keep the faith, then one day we too will walk barefoot on sun-bleached sand, wading in the warm blue waters of our own emotional Pacific.

Stupid Guy Quotes

*Cold are the hands of time that creep along relent-
lessly, destroying slowly but without pity that
which yesterday was young. Alone our memories resist this disintegration and grow more
lovely with the passing years. Heh! That's hard
to say with false teeth!*

★ Robert Dudley as "The Wienie King"
in *The Palm Beach Story*

*Hey, doll. Could you scare up another round for our table over
here? And tell the cook this is low-grade dog food. I've had better food at the ball game, you know? This steak still has marks
from where the jockey was hitting it.*

★ Rodney Dangerfield as Al Czervik in *Caddyshack*

■ **The Fugitive** (1993)
Stars: Harrison Ford, Tommy Lee Jones, Sela Ward
Director: Andrew Davis
Writers: Jeb Stuart, David Twohy, based on the TV series by Roy Huggins

Dr. Richard Kimble (Harrison Ford) is wrongly convicted of the murder of his wife
(Sela Ward). As a consequence of this gross injustice, he has to break loose of his chains,
dive out of the way of a speeding locomotive, crawl through sewers, get disentangled from
the Chicago St. Patrick's Day parade, jump into a waterfall that makes Niagara look like a
trickle, and solve the entire case by himself, all the while outwitting a relentless archneme-
sis, U.S. Marshal Samuel Gerard (Tommy Lee Jones). Really, Kimble should've just hired
the Dream Team—it would've been a lot less exhausting.

The breathlessly paced chase scene between Harrison Ford and Tommy Lee Jones does eventually wind its way back to the whodunit plot, and the denouement reassures us that in the end, we'll be heard, and treated fairly—something that's rather comforting when you've been feeling doggedly pursued by injustice and misunderstanding. Watch this when you're wishing the people in your world would just simmer down and hear you out.

▪ *The Negotiator* (1998)
Stars: Samuel L. Jackson, Kevin Spacey
Director: F. Gary Gray
Writers: James DeMonaco, Kevin Fox

Lt. Danny Roman (Samuel L. Jackson) is the best hostage negotiator in Chicago, but the number-two guy, Chris Sabian (Kevin Spacey), soon has a chance to prove he's varsity too. Roman has just brilliantly ended yet another hostage situation when he's framed in a murder and police corruption case, and the only course of action he can think of is to take hostages and barricade himself inside Internal Affairs headquarters until Sabian can unearth the truth. And you thought *you'd* run out of options. Okay, so the twisted plot here has some gaping holes (do his hostages really believe he's capable of murder?), but the thrill of watching Jackson and Spacey outwit the enemy makes up for our quibbles about the script.

Watch this one and breathe a sigh of relief as you realize that however out of control you feel, there is some promise of justice prevailing, and meanwhile, at least you haven't gone completely postal.

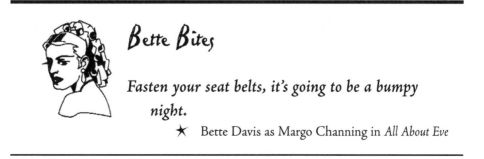

Bette Bites

Fasten your seat belts, it's going to be a bumpy night.

★　Bette Davis as Margo Channing in *All About Eve*

The "Fairer" Sex

Mr. Allen, this may come as a surprise to you, but there are some men who don't end every sentence with a proposition.

★ Doris Day as Jan Morrow in *Pillow Talk*

That cynicism you refer to I acquired the day I discovered I was different from little boys.

★ Celeste Holm as Karen in *All About Eve*

Personally, I think alligators have the right idea. They eat their young.

★ Eve Arden as Ida Corwin in *Mildred Pierce*

■ *Pacific Heights* (1990)
Stars: Michael Keaton, Melanie Griffith, Jeff Daniels
Director: John Schlesinger
Writer: Daniel Pyne

Patty (Melanie Griffith) and Drake (Jeff Daniels) aren't exactly a couple you want to root for. They're pretty irritating in their yuppie self-centeredness, and Drake's just a little too prone to bigotry to make us feel much for him. But then they are tricked into letting Carter Hayes (Michael Keaton) move into their new investment—a huge Victorian house in San Francisco that they can just barely afford, and our sympathies are roused, because before you know it, they've got an infestation of Brooklyn-sized cockroaches, sawing and hammering 24–7, no access to their own property, a restraining order against them, and a maniac cornering Patty and menacing her with a nail gun. And then the really bad stuff starts.

Luckily, Patty has a cooler head than Drake does and she figures out a less confrontational and far more effective way to deal with the evil Carter. Leave it to a woman, huh?

Check out *Pacific Heights* when you're feeling powerless against an insidious enemy—like, say, your neighbor—and we bet you'll feel a lot more confident that you've got some choices.

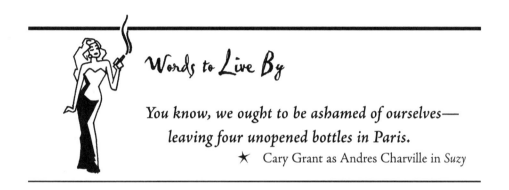

Words to Live By

You know, we ought to be ashamed of ourselves—leaving four unopened bottles in Paris.
★ Cary Grant as Andres Charville in *Suzy*

■ *The Winslow Boy* (1999)
Stars: Nigel Hawthorne, Jeremy Northam, Rebecca Pidgeon
Director: David Mamet
Writers: Terence Rattigan, David Mamet

Arthur Winslow (Nigel Hawthorne), an aging patriarch of an upper-middle-class Victorian family, is outraged when his young son is sacked from military school for allegedly cashing a postal money order that wasn't his. Ronnie (Guy Edwards II), who is the picture of prepubescent English male purity, insists upon his innocence. And his family believes him. His father and his sister Catherine (Rebecca Pidgeon), a fetching but resolute suffragette, spend every last cent in their personal purse to clear the family name and let right be done.

Into their lives comes Sir Robert Morton (Jeremy Northam), the Leslie Abramson of the Victorian period, who champions their cause at the House of Lords, restoring the blush to the Winslow rose and capturing Catherine's heart in the process. Despite the fact that one should generally worry when one's best friend is one's lawyer, this movie about a turn-of-the-twentieth-century cause célèbre reminds us that where justice is concerned, there is no such thing as chump change. And in this movie, the underdog exacts every last penny.

■ *The Solid Gold Cadillac* (1956)
Stars: Judy Holliday, Paul Douglas
Director: Richard Quine
Writer: Abe Burrows, from the play by George S. Kaufman and
    Howard Teichmann

Feeling like a victim of the big bad corporation? Tired of passing the same multinational, faceless companies on every block and still being unable to find reasonably priced, quality merchandise that's not made by virtual slaves in some Third World country—or by underpaid American schmucks like you? Then sit back and enjoy *The Solid Gold Cadillac*, the tale of a stockholder, Laura Partridge (Judy Holliday), armed with a mere ten shares of International Projects, who chooses to speak up and make a difference, and gets rewarded but good.

At the annual meeting for the public, Laura interrupts to ask: why do the do-nothings who merely attend a handful of board meetings think they're entitled to make more money than any of us will earn in ten years? The big boys fumble about with lame excuses, and eventually try to shut Laura up by giving her a desk, a secretary, and a do-nothing job of her own. But unlike her bosses, Laura actually has a work ethic. Next thing you know she's firing off letters, making friends in high and low places, and actually setting herself up to take over the company. Oh, and the one nice guy who actually accomplishes something during the workday (Paul Douglas) naturally falls madly in love with her.

Watch this movie when you're feeling overlooked and unheard and in need of some validation, and you'll feel ready to inherit the earth—even if it does require you to take charge.

> ⚠️ Warning Label: *There are some outrageously sexist lines in this prefeminist script, but let them pass you by like so many meaningless memos from that do-nothing executive who makes your work life hell.*

Reel to Real

No dumb blonde, Judy Holliday was grilled by the House Un-American Activities Committee and after *The Solid Gold Cadillac*, Hollywood refused to hire her for another film for four years.

■ *In This Our Life* (1942)
   *Stars: Olivia de Havilland, Bette Davis,
      Dennis Morgan, George Brent*
   Director: John Huston
   Writer: Howard Koch, based on the novel by Ellen Glasgow

They say Miss Stanley takes after the Fitzroy side of the family—you know, the side that embezzles, backstabs, lies through their teeth, and engages in manipulative flirtations with skeevy old uncles. Of course, she's played by Bette Davis. Meanwhile, her sister Roy, who takes after the Livingston side, has her husband (Dennis Morgan) stolen away by that scheming, betraying Stanley, and gives up without a fight or as much as a broken piece of crockery or a four-letter word, preferring to remain the quiet and dignified loser. Of course, she's played by Olivia de Havilland.

But in this morality play, Bette Davis will pay for her wide-eyed histrionics, even if she doesn't have to pay for the way-over-the-top acting. And her sis, who has the patience of Job, will prove that slow and steady wins the race. Yes, in this flick, the selfish are severely punished, the good girls find true love, civil rights lawyers are rewarded, greedy capitalists are stricken down, and a young African American man unjustly accused of a crime against a white woman in a small Southern town in the fifties sails out of jail when the cops realize he's telling the truth. Just like in real life, huh?

Wishing you could enjoy perfect justice here on earth? Forget Court TV and Judge Judy. *In This Our Life* will give you a cozy feeling that all is right with the world (although if you can't help but admire Bette Davis at her bad-girl best, we're sure you'll be forgiven).

Chapter 13

It Ain't Over 'Til the Fat Lady Yodels: Midlife Crisis Movies

Are you feeling like a 56K in a broadband world? Are the forces of gravity and hormones weighing down your desirability quotient?

If you're feeling that time keeps on slipping into the future before you've had a chance to enjoy your share of the American pie, watch one of these Midlife Crisis Movies about over-the-hill heroines who have reawakened in the middle of their lives to a whole new world of possibilities. They'll reassure you that all you have to do to join the parade that is passing you by is pick up your baton and start marching to your own drummer.

■ *Auntie Mame* (1958)
  Stars: Rosalind Russell, Forrest Tucker, Coral Browne, Peggy Cass,
      Roger Smith, Jan Handzlik
  Director: Morton DaCosta
  Writers: Betty Comden, Adolph Green, based on the novel by
      Patrick Dennis

Nobody does fabulous after forty quite like Mame Dennis (Rosalind Russell), Patrick Dennis's beloved Bohemian aunt who is the personification of bathtub-gin-fueled joie de vivre.

Mame is a socialite living in a grand pied-à-terre on Sutton Place during the Roaring Twenties. Her life is one long and eclectic cocktail party until her nephew Patrick (Jan Handzlik, Roger Smith) is orphaned and comes to live with her. Patrick must learn from Mame to stretch beyond the limitations of his staid upbringing and embrace an ever-changing world of paper wealth, free love, and the first stirrings of popular Freudian theory. Mame's world comes tumbling down around her Asian-inspired sequined slippers when the stock market crashes and she is forced to actually get a job. She discovers she has no marketable skills whatsoever—except, of course, her ineffable charm. And sure enough, despite the loss of her fortune, her complete lack of professional skills, and the Great Depression, Mame's one-hundred-proof charisma and infectious optimism overcomes every misfortune, and proves once again that women, like gin, get better with age, as long as they keep tap-dancing to that Broadway show tune in their heart.

Mame makes the experience of middle age look like sipping a perfectly chilled martini at the Plaza after a day of shopping at Bergdorf's. When you've got the midlife crisis blues, pop in *Auntie Mame*, slip on a pair of sequined slippers, and crack open the olives.

👀 *So Nice They Made It Twice:* If you're into large production numbers with Lucille Ball in a hoopskirt and a chorus of impeccably coiffed guys in red riding jackets with riding crops in their hands doing a kick line behind her, then check out the 1974 version, *Mame.*

■ *Summertime* (1955)
Stars: Katharine Hepburn, Rossano Brazzi
Director: David Lean
Writers: H. E. Bates, David Lean, based on the play
    The Time of the Cuckoo *by Arthur Laurents*

Let's face it: when you're feeling plain and unloved, as if life is passing you by, there's no one like an exuberant, middle-aged Katharine Hepburn to breathe hope back into you. And in this movie, our Kate is particularly engaged by the magic of it all as she strolls around Venice, savoring the sights, befriending the quintessential street urchin (*"Ladee! Ladee! You gotta cigaretta? Justa one-a, please!"*), flirting with a dashing local antiques dealer, and getting just a little teary over her lack of a gondola partner. But just when you're starting to feel cross with her about her desperation to be in any relationship, no matter how bad, she bucks up like the Kate we all know and love. *Prego, prego!* she tells herself. And we know that this aging Akron flower will find the romance and passion she sorely lacks—Venice will do that to ya. Well, it helps to have a good-looking Italian (Rossano Brazzi) who remembers that you adore gardenias—and who's got an "understanding" with his wife.

So why spend the money and suffer the rank stench of the polluted canals when you can enjoy a Venetian affair in Technicolor, in the privacy of your own reasonably sanitary home? Besides, you won't have to worry about any messy emotional and moral consequences afterward.

Ladies, you have to be strong and independent, and remember, don't get mad, get everything.

★ Ivana Trump as herself in *The First Wives Club*

When Can We Move In?: Cinema Apartments We Covet

We have turned to movies for models of inspiring behavior, examples of triumphing over formidable odds, and insight into the conundrums of our lives. But sometimes while watching a movie, we keep getting distracted with one compelling question: "Where can I find a mind-blowing apartment like that on my budget?" Here are just a few of the delightfully decadent dwellings we've lusted over on the screen as we wait in our cramped walk-ups for the landlord to fix the boiler yet again.

Easy Living (1937)

The sable coat that drops on Mary Smith's (Jean Arthur) head is nice and all, but it's the hotel room that drops into her lap that we salivate over. All white, all art deco—and that living room! Does one drape one's self on the chaise, or take a seat at the creamy grand piano and compose whilst gazing at the vase of calla lilies, or does one stand on the double-tiered semicircle riser by the window and look out across that magnificent Manhattan skyline—and muse about ways to prevent the Donald Trumps of the world from ruining the view with their tacky phallic odes to ego? Ah, but the zenith of this hotel suite is that scalloped fountain with a Greek statue overseeing one's little dip. No matter what our cares, we could certainly wash them away with a frolic in this utterly frivolous bit of plumbing!

Two Girls and a Guy (1997)

In this drama about two women who discover they have the same boyfriend, the main character, played by Robert Downey, Jr., is supposed to

. . . continued

be a marginally employed actor, but he can afford payments on a sunny, airy, hardwood-floored, full-windowed, kitchen-nooked, high-ceilinged, split-level Soho loft decorated in a minimalist style with Scandinavian design furniture and a grand piano. Hey, if that's not a sure sign that he's hiding something, we don't know what is. We couldn't stand the obnoxious guy-centric story in this flick, but all that exquisite square footage had us mesmerized.

Stigmata (1999)

Let's see—a humongous studio with a raised platform for the bed, an antique tub, gigantic windows, and the traditional alphabet-city decor of mannequins, inflatable furniture, and little tables piled high with thick drippy candles, that a hairdresser on Manhattan's Lower East Side can afford? We'd love to take over her lease! However, we would probably want to install a little track lighting to brighten the place up, wipe the bloodstains off the floor, do a little sponge painting over the gibberish the previous tenant scrawled all over the west wall while possessed, and banish the malevolent spirit that keeps trashing the place.

Big (1988)

Actually, we covet two apartments in this movie: when we're in a wine-and-cheese mood, we'll take the airy partitioned apartment that belongs to Susan (Elizabeth Perkins), which comes complete with shabby chic wardrobe and leather couch. And for those times when we want to pig out on Oreos and beer, we'll take the huge warehouse-district loft with all-hardwood floors, ample closet space, Jacuzzi, and endless windows that belongs to Josh (Tom Hanks)—and is filled with pinball machines, blow-up Godzillas, and a trampoline.

■ *The Secret Life of Girls* (1999) (*also known as* American Pie)
Stars: Majandra Delfino, Linda Hamilton, Eugene Levy
Director and Writer: Holly Goldberg Sloan

Dealing with a midlife breakup that's left you unmoored? Here's a movie that will have you laughing about how we all have to go a little crazy with grief sometimes in order to re-claim ourselves and discover a new and more rewarding path.

In this dead-on comedy set in Oregon in the seventies, where Bradyesque ranch houses are all the rage and divorce among the white middle class is as common as hideous home decor, Hugh Sanford (Eugene Levy) is a college professor with an appalling fashion sense (white guys in dashikis—it's a wonder America survived). When he dumps his wife, Ruby (Linda Hamilton), for a grad student, Ruby enters a state of rage that has her obsessively investigating her rival one day and selling off all of Hugh's possessions at a garage sale the next. Caught in the middle is the Sanfords' intellectually precocious daughter Natalie (Ma-jandra Delfino), who really just wants her mother to get off her yearlong crying jag and jeal-ous rampage, and her father to stop acting like a jerk, so that she can get on with being a teenager. Helping Natalie to feel even more isolated and confused by it all is her airhead friend Kay (Meagan Good), who is less interested in trying to make sense of a psychologically complex world than in trying out that new spray-on shampoo for girls on the go.

In the end, Ruby discovers that, just like the beautiful antique wooden staircase she stores in her garage, life doesn't have to have a defined destination to be fulfilling. We dis-cover along with Natalie that the Marcia Bradys of the world don't always fare better than the Jans, and we learn that no matter how old we are, we are all prone to growing pains.

When you're halfway through your life plan and things aren't adding up as you ex-pected, *The Secret Life of Girls* is a wonderful reminder that chaos can lead to rebirth, reju-venation, and a fabulous new decorating scheme. So put his stuff up on eBay, invest in a few antique pieces for yourself, and tell yourself that in the end, you'll get to where you're meant to be so you might as well enjoy the journey.

■ *Sweet Bird of Youth* (1989)

Stars: Elizabeth Taylor, Mark Harmon
Director: Nicholas Roeg
Writers: Gavin Lambert, based on the play by Tennessee Williams

Elizabeth Taylor stars as yet another exceedingly well-scripted, drunken, blowsy, sharp-tongued, evil-spirited, self-centered, middle-aged bitch goddess whom we just can't help but fall in love with. Alexandra Del Lago (Elizabeth Taylor) is an aging screen star who picks up Chance Wayne (Mark Harmon), a massage therapist/gigolo who dreams of becoming a movie star. Chance is bent on using "the Princess" to get him a screen test in Hollywood in exchange for sexual favors.

Instead of heading straight for Hollywood and Vine, however, Chance and the Princess head for Chance's hometown of St. Cloud, Louisiana, where he left his heart, and his integrity, many years before. And as we have come to expect from Tennessee Williams, what results is a lush and poetic antebellum revenge tragedy that condemns the guilty, forever tarnishes the innocent, and rewards the bitch.

When you're feeling like everything that's going to happen to you has already happened, spend a few hours with Chance and the Princess, who remind us that no matter how glorious we were in our prime, we have to find a way to accept that our youth is over—and that's not such a terrible thing.

👁👁 *So Nice They Made It Twice:* The original version of this movie with Paul Newman and Geraldine Page is also a faithful and substantive adaptation of Tennessee Williams's play, although in this version Paul Newman's Chance totally upstages Page's fading princess of the silver screen. We prefer the remake because, with all due respect to Geraldine Page, nobody can do blowsy but irresistible and totally inebriated narcissism quite like Ms. Liz.

Lethal Liz Lines

By the time I was your age, I was already a legend.
★ Elizabeth Taylor as Alexandra Del Lago
in *Sweet Bird of Youth*

When monster meets monster, one of them has to give way. And it will never be me. I'm an older hand at it.

★ Elizabeth Taylor as Alexandra Del Lago in *Sweet Bird of Youth*

Legends don't die easily. They hang on long. And their vanity is infinite.

★ Elizabeth Taylor as Alexandra Del Lago in *Sweet Bird of Youth*

■ *Peggy Sue Got Married* (1986)
Stars: Kathleen Turner, Nicolas Cage
Director: Francis Ford Coppola
Writers: Jerry Leichtling, Arlene Sarner

There's so much she would change if only she could go back—the marriage that became the scapegoat for their disappointments, her inattention to the important female relationships in her life, her lack of appreciation for the simplicity of life in the late 1950s, and especially the lost chance to get horizontal with that passionate guy with the motorcycle, black turtleneck, and penchant for quoting *On the Road*. Yeah, so he turned out to be just another self-centered Kerouac wannabe who dreamed of settling down in Utah with two wives and a chicken farm. But what a glorious night under the stars she could've had!

Through the magic of a vaguely explained heart ailment combined with a fainting spell, Peggy Sue (Kathleen Turner) is able to return to her senior year of high school. To her dismay, she finds herself compelled to reengage with her soon-to-be ex-husband, Crazy Charlie the Appliance King (Nicolas Cage, with a ridiculous pompadour and an even more ridiculous nasal accent). Back then, Charlie had the car, the gold lamé jacket, and the do, and he aspired to be the next Dion. This time around, Peggy Sue pushes him to follow his dreams so he won't hang his disappointments on her. But as she comes to discover, we come to be who we are only by traveling the road we traveled, and much as we'd love to avoid the potholes, wrong turns, broken pavement, and "scenic" routes through the warehouse district, all destinies require a certain amount of four-wheeling.

Watch this one when you're tempted to give in to regrets and you'll start believing that you followed the right path after all.

■ *American Beauty* (1999)
Stars: Kevin Spacey, Annette Bening, Thora Birch, Wes Bentley, Mena Suvari
Director: Sam Mendes
Writer: Alan Ball

There's nothing like a voice from the grave to remind us to live life to the fullest, and stop and gather our rose petals while we may.

In *American Beauty*, Kevin Spacey stars as Lester Burnham, a disgruntled idealist who wakes up from the coma of compliant middle age, sheds his excess baggage and his spare tire, tells off his boss as well as his manic wife (Annette Bening), and rediscovers the beauty of life, physical fitness, and saucy pubescent cheerleaders. While on the surface this might seem like a movie that glorifies the rapacious appetites of a male in midlife crisis—after all, Lester falls in love with a teenage cheerleader and starts smoking a lot of high-octane pot—what actually occurs is a reawakening of the senses that invites us all to look deeper at the world around us, and glimpse the exquisitely painful beauty of life.

Before you tell the world to stick a fork in you and turn you over because you're done, watch *American Beauty* and remember that it's never too late to surprise yourself.

World-Class Wrecks

Brandon is the sort of man everyone speaks well of, but nobody talks to.
★ Greg Wise as John Willoughby in *Sense and Sensibility*

You don't frighten us, English pig dogs! Go and boil your bottoms, you sons of a silly person!
★ John Cleese as the French Guard in *Monty Python and the Holy Grail*

Stupid Guy Quotes

The first line I ever wrote was "I am an antichrist" but I couldn't think of anything that rhymed with it.

★ Johnny Rotten (John Lydon) in *The Filth and the Fury*

■ *Music of the Heart* (1999)
Stars: Meryl Streep, Angela Bassett, Aidan Quinn
Director: Wes Craven
Writer: Pamela Gray, based on "Small Wonders," a documentary of the life story of Roberta Guaspari

Roberta (Meryl Streep) is an unemployed single mom whose husband has just run off with her friend Lana. To make matters worse, the movers are manhandling her prized possessions, reducing her to a weepy mess whose life is literally and figuratively stuck on hold. And she's wearing a drab men's gray plaid bathrobe—hardly the uniform of a woman in charge of her own destiny. Clearly, Roberta needs a shot of self-esteem, a sense of entitlement, a reasonable divorce settlement, and a silk embroidered peignoir in a cheerful color that'll make those dark moments of despair at least a little more tolerable. Hey, if you're gonna mope, you might as well look fabulous doing it, right?

But while Roberta may be down, she's not out for the count. Sure, her résumé contains far too much white space to impress potential employers, but she's got a string of fake pearls, plenty o' spunk, and enough confidence in her talents as a teacher to convince a local school principal (Angela Bassett) to give her a chance. She starts a program to teach violin to inner-city students, and as the program blossoms, so does Roberta. Suddenly, she recognizes that she doesn't need to settle anymore—for half-out-of-it home contractors or for half-baked relationships. What's more, she comes to value her own gifts—including her lovably cranky and forthright persona—and the world comes to value them as well.

Music of the Heart is the perfect movie for when you're at a crossroads and feeling grumpy, lumpy, and underappreciated. Who knows—maybe it'll get your entrepreneurial blood rushing, or at least inspire you to trade in your terry cloth for silk and lace.

World-Class Rants

Now, I ask you, Duarto, who's supposed to wear that? Some anorexic teenager? Some fetus? It's a conspiracy, I know it is! I've had enough. I'm leading a protest. I'm not buying another article of clothing until these designers come to their senses.

★ Bette Midler as Brenda in *The First Wives Club*

The whole purpose of places like Starbucks is for people with no decision-making ability whatsoever to make six decisions just to buy one cup of coffee. Short, tall, light, dark, caf, decaf, lowfat, nonfat, etc. So people who don't know what the hell they're doing or who on earth they are can, for only $2.95, get not just a cup of coffee but an absolutely defining sense of self: Tall! Decaf! Cappuccino!

★ Tom Hanks as Joe Fox III in *You've Got Mail*

Gifford's a sap, that's what Gifford is. I'd give him away with a spray of horseradish. I wouldn't be caught dead with him in a duckboat, and if you're a lady and they're gentlemen, I'm Amy Semple McCotton on a raft. You can take your Bostons and your Bunker Hills and your bloodlines and stuff a codfish with them, and then you know what you can do with the codfish.

★ Jean Harlow as Lola Burns in *Bombshell*

■ *Ash Wednesday* (1973)
Stars: Elizabeth Taylor, Henry Fonda
Director: Larry Peerce
Writer: Jean-Claude Tramont

Thinking that a few nips and tucks, and a little fat-cell-vacuuming will solve your midlife crisis? Well, as Detroit homemaker Barbara Sawyer (Elizabeth Taylor) discovers, cosmetic surgery may give you that Vaseline-over-the-lens luminescence, but reversing the march of time on your face, thighs, and belly is very different from reversing the march of time on your relationship.

Hubby Mark (Henry Fonda) is having an affair with a woman younger than his own daughter and Barbara thinks that if she goes under the knife she can win back his heart. And who can blame her for hoping after investing more than thirty years in their marriage? Barbara's physical transformation is astonishing—oh, to look like the violet-eyed Liz in her prime! Moreover, her postmakeover wardrobe is too fabulous for words: it's almost enough to make you run out and buy your own turban-and-fur ensemble. But the gruesomeness of the surgery itself, performed in secrecy in an era when such things weren't discussed openly in *People* magazine, not to mention her painful physical recovery, makes you realize just how sad it is that Barbara is so desperate to reverse time. In the end, Barbara undergoes a transformation that is far more empowering than cosmetic, and far more natural than having her cheeks pulled back to her ears.

Watch this one when you want to be reminded that change is your friend.

Facing Facts

This dress exacerbates the genetic betrayal that is my legacy.

★ Janeane Garofalo as Heather Mooney
in *Romy and Michele's High School Reunion*

■ *Saving Grace* (2000)
Stars: Brenda Blethyn, Craig Ferguson, Valerie Edmond
Director: Nigel Cole
Writers: Mark Crowdy, Craig Ferguson

When her husband jumps out of an airplane without a parachute and plunges to his death, middle-aged Grace (Brenda Blethyn) is left with a mountain of unpaid bills, a home mortgaged to the hilt, and absolutely no marketable skills with which to dig herself out. Except, of course, her uncanny knack for nurturing exotic plants in her greenhouse. Forced to come up with a large sum of money to save her home and her lifestyle, Grace uses her green thumb to cultivate contraband, and in the process, produces a bumper crop of self-reliance. Soon Grace finds herself thrust into the brave new world outside her climate-controlled hothouse reality, and discovers that loss is just nature's way of making room for new things to grow.

When you feel like the support systems in your life have taken a swan dive, watch *Saving Grace* and remember that it's never too late to sprout wings, or shake a tail feather.

You Go, Girl

Well, we went skinny-dipping and we did things that frightened the fish.

★ Julia Roberts as Shelby in *Steel Magnolias*

■ *Shirley Valentine* (1989)
Stars: Pauline Collins, Tom Conti, Bernard Hill
Director: Lewis Gilbert
Writer: Willy Russell, based on his play

Shirley Valentine Bradshaw (Pauline Collins) is trapped in the role of middle-class British housewife, married to a man (Bernard Hill) whose playfulness and flirtatiousness have degenerated into one-syllable demands and grunts. As for passion, Shirley grumbles, "I think sex is like supermarkets—you know, overrated. Just a lot of pushing and shoving and you still come out with very little at the end."

For all her flippant comments, though, Shirley is starting to realize she's lost a precious part of herself somewhere along the way. Her chance for renewal comes in the form of a ticket to Greece, where Shirley can sit on a beach, sip the local wine, look out at the ocean, and rediscover her sexual response with the help of a local innkeeper (Tom Conti), who has a boat just the right size for an afternoon of jumping feet first into oceans of sensuality.

No longer "Shirley Bradshaw, middle-aged housewife beginning to sag a bit," she becomes "Shirley the Brave, Shirley the Marvelous . . . Shirley Valentine!" And if her husband, Joe, wants her back, he's going to have to meet her on her terms and buy his own damn ticket to paradise.

When you find that you have your best conversations with a wall, your unflappable and brave younger self seems like a dream child that got lost somewhere around the time that Tuesdays petrified into steak-and-potatoes night, and your lingerie drawer is filled with sensible underwear, *Shirley Valentine* is the perfect tonic.

Pearls from Pauline

I'm not sayin' she's a bragger, but if you've been to Paradise, she's got a season ticket. She's that type, Gillian, you know. If you've got a headache, she's got a brain tumor.

★ Pauline Collins as *Shirley Valentine*

I'm goin' to Greece for the sex. Sex for breakfast, sex for dinner, sex for tea, and sex for supper.

★ Pauline Collins as *Shirley Valentine*

■ *The School of Flesh* (1998)

Stars: Isabelle Huppert, Vincent Martinez, Vincent Lindon,
  Marthe Keller
Director: Benoît Jacquot
Writer: Jacques Fieschi, based on the novel by Yukio Mishima

Dominique (Isabelle Huppert), a middle-aged fashion executive in search of sensation, becomes obsessed with a staggeringly handsome bisexual bartender named Quentin (Vincent Martinez), who moonlights as a hustler and as a kickboxer (how's that for a résumé?). Despite her better instincts, Dominique cannot rest until she possesses Quentin, and the two begin a complicated, largely verbal, and extremely French love affair, as they duel for power and control over such imperative French issues as which fork to use with the fish.

When you're feeling bored with the same old tried and true, watch *The School of Flesh* and indulge in an obsessive, control-driven love affair with a sexually ambiguous, much younger kickboxer with very poor table manners—without having to pick up the bar tab or wear protective gear.

Chapter 14

You Go, Girlfriend!: Role Model Movies

Not every woman can be the queen of England, or a legendary pop singer, or the official saint of her native country. Most of us lead far simpler lives with less predictable conflicts and resolutions—and far less fabulous costuming and cinematography—than Hollywood offers us. But the movies in this chapter show that when a woman truly knows herself, and has the courage to follow her own path, she can face anything from an invading army to a judgmental community to a car salesman getting downright snippy—and demand her due.

If you're feeling like a boot scrape in the portico of life, it might be time to pick yourself up off of the floor, dust yourself off, and watch one of these Role Model Movies about heroines who find their place in the sun and spring into full blossom in a garden of their own making.

■ *Elizabeth* (1998)

Stars: Cate Blanchett, Joseph Fiennes, Geoffrey Rush
Director: Shekhar Kapur
Writer: Michael Hirst

Elizabeth tells the story of the early years of the reign of Elizabeth I of England, who learns the hard way that marriage and monarchy do not mix.

Cate Blanchett stars as the Protestant virgin queen, who, after the death of her Catholic half-sister, Queen Mary, succeeds to the throne only to fend off intrigues at every turn from enemies bent on murdering her in order to return the throne to the Catholics. Her Protestant supporters, on the other hand, are anxious for Elizabeth to marry and produce an heir to secure the throne for them. Elizabeth learns that she can't please all of the people all of the time, and that goes double for husbands and paramours, who assert their male dominance by conspiring with her assassins.

When your court conspirators are closing in and threatening to topple your throne, let Elizabeth remind you that while it can be lonely at the top, if you expect to remain the undisputed queen of your realm, sometimes you have to be willing to rule alone.

☀ Reel to Real

If you go by the replica at the Brading Wax Museum on the Isle of Wight of how Elizabeth I might have actually looked, she didn't resemble the ethereal Cate Blanchett with that crème fraîche complexion and cloud of red curls so much as Ethel Merman in her dotage. There are a lot of portraits of Elizabeth, however, in which she looks extraordinarily fetching, but we suspect these painters were on the payroll. Still, all in all, you do have to hand it to a woman who can make ruffs, a receding hairline, and virginity fashionable through the power of her personality.

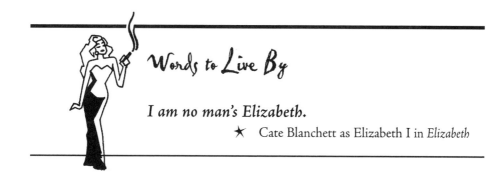

Words to Live By

I am no man's Elizabeth.

★ Cate Blanchett as Elizabeth I in *Elizabeth*

■ *Fargo* (1996)
Stars: Frances McDormand, William H. Macy, Steve Buscemi, Peter Stormare
Director: Joel Coen
Writers: Joel Coen, Ethan Coen

Standing against the starkness of an empty and vast snow-covered field of moral uncertainty is Marge Gunderson (Frances McDormand), a clear-cut figure of goodness, honesty, and the work ethic, and a symbol of the enduring practicality of feminine intuition—not to mention earflap caps in northern Minnesota.

Anyway, Marge, a cop in a remote rural area not far from the Twin Cities, believes that people always come before profit. She's the kind of gal who thinks that an excruciatingly awkward lunch date with an old acquaintance who is getting kinda creepy on her is a small price to pay to make someone's day just a little brighter. She knows the value of an all-you-can-eat buffet. And she recognizes one very simple truth: there is never, *never* any call to get snippy.

But to Marge's shock and horror, she soon finds herself on the trail of a sociopath named Gaear Grimsrud (Peter Stormare) and his slimy and barely competent (albeit screamingly funny) accomplice Carl Showalter (Steve Buscemi). Grimsrud and Showalter have bungled a moneymaking scheme dreamed up by a frightened and desperate little man named Jerry Lundegaard (William H. Macy), who is a mere eighty-nine-cent ice scraper in a world of endless frost. Fearlessly, Marge follows her instincts and closes in on the criminals. Will an honest, smart, brave, and intuitive woman bent on achieving justice triumph over evil and greed? *Oh, jah, you betcha.*

Feeling ordinary and invisible lately? Spend a couple of hours cheering on Marge, a true original, as she tries to collar her perps, and enjoy watching a woman who isn't young, glamorous, or living in a major urban center save the day.

> ⚠️ **Warning Label:** *The black humor of the Coen brothers can be very upsetting for some, especially when the cartoon violence takes a sinister turn.*

Nancy's Momentous Minutiae: Renaissance Women

Joan Fontaine is not only an Academy Award–winning actress, she is also an excellent horsewoman, a prizewinning angler, a hole-in-one golfer, a fantastic cook, a licensed interior decorator, and a pilot to boot.

Shirley Temple was the top Hollywood box office champ for three years in a row during the Depression, despite the fact that her age was in the single digits. She later went on to become the U.S. ambassador to Ghana and Czechoslovakia and was one of the very first public figures to publicly discuss having had breast cancer.

Butterfly McQueen, who played the simpleminded Prissy in *Gone With the Wind*, had a B.A. in political science and was a community activist in Harlem.

■ *The Messenger* (1999)
Stars: Milla Jovovich, Dustin Hoffman, Faye Dunaway, John Malkovich
Director: Luc Besson
Writers: Luc Besson, Andrew Birkin

This is the supermodel-as-saint version of the legendary story of Jeanne D'Arc, the young French girl who sees her first vision at age thirteen. Joan of Arc (Milla Jovovich) leads an army to victory for the Dauphin at eighteen only to be burned alive in the marketplace one year later.

Okay, so a martyred saint who hears divine command voices and never sees the other side of twenty is not exactly a role model that we modern women can immediately relate to. And then you cast her with a supermodel and one would think that the chasm would really start to yawn. But this version of the Lark of Domremy is like the action adventure Saint Joan, and actually interprets her as a heroine of the new millennium that we can relate to. This Joan gets to slap on armor, wield a really cool broadsword, leap over moats on horseback, and sport an adorable but androgynous Calvin Klein–inspired hairdo. And she has this really cute aide-de-camp who obeys her every command.

Watch this movie when you're feeling like a martyr tied to the stake of life, and let Joan teach you that when you feel your cause is just, and your vision true, you should listen to those voices in your head telling you to storm the nearest citadel.

Bods We Don't Buy

Movies can teach us a lot about ourselves, but when it comes to presenting images of women's bodies, they can get downright surreal. Here are some cinematic bods we just don't buy.

Helen Hunt in *Pay It Forward*
Hunt is supposedly an over-thirty woman who's got a kid and a serious drinking problem, and yet she's skinny enough to have a jutting collarbone and legs that look like they've been sculpted by a combination of Tae-Bo and kickboxing. Sheesh, maybe we should take to downing fifths of vodka every day.

Gwyneth Paltrow in *Hush*
A few hours after giving birth and being drugged up with class-one narcotics, she's freshly scrubbed and practically glowing, not to mention flat-

. . . continued

bellied. And she practically skips into the kitchen for breakfast, clearly un-hampered by maxipads. Boy, do we wish.

Milla Jovovich in *The Messenger*

It's not enough that we risk our lives in combat and sacrifice ourselves for the future of our native country. Nooooo. We have to be just shy of six feet tall, a good thirty pounds under the average, and have a flawless complexion and high cheekbones, too.

And while we're at it, we'd just like to know:

How come missionary Gladys Aylward (Ingrid Bergman in *The Inn of the Sixth Happiness*), who lives in an obscure province of China in the 1930s, has access to a Hollywood stylist, curlers, makeup, and a manicurist?

How does advertising exec Darcy McGuire (Helen Hunt in *What Women Want*) get away with wearing a bateau neckline sweater the first day on the job, and a powder-blue sleeveless microminidress in a pitch meeting with clients, when she works for a male-dominated company in the conservative city of Chicago?

How many streetwalking prostitutes have the long, lean, toned legs and perfect teeth and complexion of Julia Roberts in *Pretty Woman?*

▪ *The Inn of the Sixth Happiness* (1958)

Stars: Ingrid Bergman, Curt Jürgens, Robert Donat, Moultrie Kelsall
Director: Mark Robson
Writer: Isobel Lennart, based on the book The Small Woman,
    by Alan Burgess

Back in the era before missionary zeal was politically suspect, Ingrid Bergman re-deemed herself in the eyes of Hollywood's moralists (having left her husband for another man and earned their wrath) in this inspiring story of a real-life woman who had an unshakable sense of destiny and an attitude that demanded respect.

Gladys Aylward (Ingrid Bergman) is obsessed with going to pre–Maoist China to spread the word of God and help the people however she can, but she's told by the head of the China Missionary Society in London (Moultrie Kelsall as Dr. Robinson) that she has nothing to offer. Famous last words—don't worry, he gets his in the last reel. Anyway, within a few months, Gladys has saved enough pennies to travel to a remote village in northern China, where she begins working at a small inn. Before long she's making sure the local women cease binding the feet of their daughters and granddaughters, stopping a prison riot, agitating the local laborers, adopting a handful of orphans, spreading literacy to the provinces—and that's just in her spare time. Driven with a desire to "make each man know that he counts, whether he believes in Christ or Buddha or nothing," she refuses to stop her work for minor distractions like a Hollywoodized love interest (Curt Jürgens) or the invading Japanese army.

Watch this one when you're tired of people scoffing at your dreams and underestimating your ability to make things happen. Gladys shows us that when you are true to yourself, you will find the courage to do what has to be done.

> ⚠ Warning Label: *You'll have to overlook some of that oldfashioned paternalism toward the locals, dubious messages about biracialism, and the distraction of Bergman's ever-perfect coif, but we think that whatever your politics, you'll find yourself rooting for Gladys and just waiting for that naysayer at the Missionary Society to eat his words.*

🎥 Reel to Real

The real-life Gladys Aylward managed to accomplish everything Ingrid Bergman did in the movie, including marching one hundred orphans for twelve days through the mountains to escape the invading Japanese army, and then some.

Hoopskirt Nightmares

Hey, we're hardly the arbiters of fashion, being partial to unstructured tops and boots actually made for walking, but these movies made us want to phone the fashion police ourselves and press charges.

Autumn in New York (2000)

Winona Ryder's character makes whimsical hats that she claims "capture the line of a woman's waist," but to us they look like those deely-bopper antennae thingies we bought at the Wisconsin State Fair in the eighties.

Brazil (1985)

It's hard to recall much about this confusing film, but if you've seen it, we bet you remember the hat, don't you? It appeared in a scene pivotal to the plot and we got all confused because we couldn't stop staring at that upside-down-overshoe-shaped chapeau. Truly the most distracting and ridiculous fashion in modern cinema (okay, we did giggle ourselves silly, though).

Pride and Prejudice (1940)

The 1930s- and 1940s-era obnoxious fabrics (*plaids?* Elizabeth Bennet in *plaids?*) are bad enough, but instead of Grecian-inspired, empire-waisted dresses typical of the early nineteenth century, Greer Garson and her cinematic sisters flounce about in Civil War–era hoopskirts. Somehow, we don't picture the Bennet girls as forty years ahead of Paris!

. . . continued

Sabrina (1995)

A costume-flick remake gone disastrously awry. Sabrina's ever-so-chic jumpsuit is transformed into a T-shirt and jumper combo that holds no charm whatsoever; her evening gowns are more Staten Island than Manhattan; and the Long Island ladies who lunch appear to be wearing Christian LaCroix knockoffs they got off one of those tables near the registers at Costco.

■ *Funny Face* (1957)
Stars: Audrey Hepburn, Fred Astaire, Michel Auclair
Director: Stanley Donen
Writer: Leonard Gershe

In *Funny Face*, Audrey Hepburn plays Jo Stockton, a bookish, brilliant, and determined girl in a jumper and sensible shoes who only agrees to an offer to model a collection in Paris (so shallow!) because it will enable her to hang out in cafes discussing philosophy and meet Professor Émile Flostre (Michel Auclair), with whom she can discuss the implications of his pet philosophy of empathicalism. But since Fred Astaire is taking the photos, Edith Head and Givenchy are doing the costumes, Richard Avedon is helping with the visuals, and George and Ira Gershwin are writing the songs, you can guess she's going to spend a lot of time decked out in scrumptious gowns and tiaras while singing and dancing (well, okay, she's also got that jazzy bohemian number in the cafe when she's wearing a black cat suit and snapping her fingers to the bongo beat, man). But while Jo plays the role of "*Quality* magazine's fresh-faced new woman" with zest and aplomb (watch her spirited dash down the steps in front of *Winged Victory* in the Louvre), once she dons the collection's wedding gown she decides that she needs a little old-fashioned romance and domesticity to complete herself. But her man is going to have to appreciate the finer points of her personal philosophy and respect her intellect if he's going to have the privilege of walking down the aisle of a little country church with her.

If you need to believe that there are men out there who can appreciate your fabulous combo of glamour, style, and your love for obscure French philosophical theory, indulge in *Funny Face.* Because you're worth it.

You know, even though I had to wear that stupid back brace and you were kind of fat, we were still totally cutting edge.
★ Lisa Kudrow as Michele in *Romy and Michele's High School Reunion*

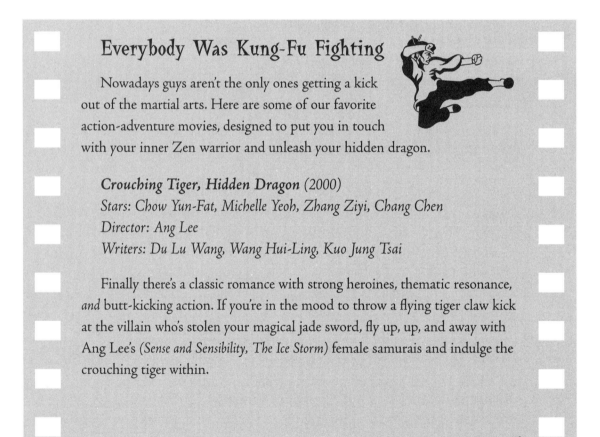

Everybody Was Kung-Fu Fighting

Nowadays guys aren't the only ones getting a kick out of the martial arts. Here are some of our favorite action-adventure movies, designed to put you in touch with your inner Zen warrior and unleash your hidden dragon.

Crouching Tiger, Hidden Dragon (2000)
Stars: Chow Yun-Fat, Michelle Yeoh, Zhang Ziyi, Chang Chen
Director: Ang Lee
Writers: Du Lu Wang, Wang Hui-Ling, Kuo Jung Tsai

Finally there's a classic romance with strong heroines, thematic resonance, *and* butt-kicking action. If you're in the mood to throw a flying tiger claw kick at the villain who's stolen your magical jade sword, fly up, up, and away with Ang Lee's (*Sense and Sensibility, The Ice Storm*) female samurais and indulge the crouching tiger within.

. . . *continued*

Shanghai Noon *(2000)*
Stars: Jackie Chan, Owen Wilson, Lucy Liu
Director: Tom Dey
Writers: Miles Millar, Alfred Gough

The martial arts meet slapstick comedy in this vehicle for the Buster Keaton of kung fu: Jackie Chan. Jackie is like a bad-hair-day action-adventure hero, who reminds us that even imperial guard rejects can prevail over the outlaws, find the stolen gold, and marry the princess by employing a series of brilliantly executed martial arts acrobatics and a good sense of humor. This movie has the added benefit of that adorable Owen Wilson as the bumbling train robber.

The Matrix *(1999)*
Stars: Keanu Reeves, Laurence Fishburne, Carrie-Anne Moss
Directors and Writers: Andy Wachowski, Larry Wachowski

Satisfy your rage against the machine with this sci-fi thriller that pits human beings against software programs—and the humans come up short. Except for one human: Neo (Keanu Reeves), a cyber-age Christ figure in a long black coat who uses the martial arts to defy gravity, physics, bandwidth, and the one-dimensional nature of action-adventure movies that substitute action for character development and plotline. Pop this one in when your emotional hard drive needs defragging, take a break from the keyboard, and spend a few hours doing the martial arts mambo with Keanu. You'll be glad you did.

▪ *Impromptu* (1991)
Stars: Judy Davis, Hugh Grant, Emma Thompson, Bernadette Peters
Director: James Lapine
Writer: Sarah Kernochan

This biographical movie about nineteenth-century author and cause célèbre George Sand reminds us that sometimes it takes a woman to walk like a man. Judy Davis stars as Sand, a nineteenth-century writer with a proclivity for wearing trousers, smoking cigars in public, pursuing men and, well, taking the name George probably didn't help her social standing much either.

While away at a salon for artists and painters held at the country estate of the pretentious Duchesse D'Antan (Emma Thompson), George Sand meets and falls passionately in love with the tubercular and frail Polish composer Frédéric Chopin (Hugh Grant). She begins a full-scale effort to woo and win Chopin, a delicate, almost ethereal creature, who has one foot in this world and one foot in the next. But George, who has both hobnail-booted feet planted firmly in the here and now, refuses to take no for an answer.

This is a great movie to watch when your esprit de corps is flagging and you need somebody like George to remind you that while life is a banquet, you've got to pick up a plate and get in the buffet line, because there is no waiter service.

Reel to Real

George Sand's real name was Amandine Aurore Lucie Dupin. She became famous in her lifetime (1804–76) for gender bending. She walked out on her aristocratic husband when she was twenty-seven, moved to Paris, wrote novels, and hung out in cafes drinking coffee with handsome intellectuals. George's insistence on "walking like a man" instead of being "ladylike" helped society become more expansive in its view of women.

Freudian Slipups

Bull Durham (1988)
Stars: Kevin Costner, Susan Sarandon, Tim Robbins
Director and Writer: Ron Shelton

On the surface, *Bull Durham* has all the earmarks of a great Role Model Movie. Annie Savoy (Susan Sarandon) is a metaphysically minded baseball fan who provides her own unique form of training to one up-and-comer on the Durham Bulls each season. Crash Davis (Kevin Costner), a veteran minor league catcher, and Ebbie Calvin "Nuke" LaLoosh (Tim Robbins), the new star rookie pitcher, both make Annie's final cut. Crash Davis refuses to bite, so Annie takes Nuke in hand and turns him into an all-star on the field and off until Crash gate-crashes at the bottom of the ninth and steals home.

While Annie Savoy is a substantive female character who uses terms like *ontological* and *quantum physics*, the sum total of the education she has to impart seems to take place in the bedroom. It is hard for us to imagine that a woman with enough mental creativity to find parallels between Walt Whitman, baseball, and life would have nothing more to offer than a good roll in the hay. We wish this movie would have focused less on what was between Annie's legs and more on what was between her ears.

Words to Live By

I could never love a Baywatch fan.
★ Gwyneth Paltrow as Helen in *Sliding Doors*

■ *Erin Brockovich* (2000)
Stars: Julia Roberts, Albert Finney, Aaron Eckhart
Director: Steven Soderbergh
Writer: Susannah Grant

Erin Brockovich's luck is running very low—she's an unemployed single mom whose child support payments have disappeared. Worse, a loud biker (Aaron Eckhart) just moved in next door, she's got a dishearteningly large credit card debt, and her open-and-shut personal injury lawsuit slammed shut without paying off in the five figures she'd hoped for. But, hey, at least she can drink her tap water without fear of reordering her DNA strands, which is more than she can say for some nice folks living near a big puddle left behind in the desert by Pacific Gas and Electric.

Having bullied her lawyer (Albert Finney) into hiring her for basic office work, Erin (Julia Roberts) stumbles across the plight of these hapless folks and, her empathy roused, becomes a one-woman Ralph Nader–cum–Rachel Carson in a push-up bra. She picks dead frogs out of the polluted pond for chemical analysis, blows away the other lawyers with her attention to detail, and finds the smoking gun they need to ensure a megasettlement.

As a whistle-blower who punishes the big bad capitalists, Erin's a woman you've got to love—even more so because she isn't the perfect mom and girlfriend. Let's face it: as all us failed superwomen know, when you're fighting for truth, justice, and the American way, something's gotta give and they're just gonna have to bear with you.

Alright, we admit you've got to put up with a few groaning points in this movie. Try to look past Julia Roberts's impossibly thin body and perfect hair that cascades over her shoulders and fairly glows in the setting sun, and imagine the real Erin Brockovich—who we like to believe is perhaps a little broad in the beam and in need of deep conditioning, particularly after spending hours in the desert collecting soil samples. And it's really annoying that all the educated women in this movie are portrayed as ugly, sexless, eggheaded losers who are jealous of their sexier, salt-of-the-earth coworker. Still, if you're willing to close your eyes to the more unsettling messages here about educated career women, *Erin Brockovich* may encourage you to face your own battles.

Pearls from Pauline

I just can't bring myself to hate people. The worse they behave, the sorrier I feel for them.

★ Pauline Collins as Margaret Drummond in *Paradise Road*

∎ *A Price Above Rubies* (1998)
  Stars: Renée Zellweger, Christopher Eccleston, Allen Payne, Julianna Margulies,
  Glenn Fitzgerald
  Director and Writer: Boaz Yakin

In the insular world of an Orthodox Jewish community somewhere in Brooklyn, Sonia Horowitz (Renée Zellweger) is doing her best to be a good wife and mom, really she is. But underneath that plain head scarf is an exceptionally quick mind, a strong will, a thirst for freedom, and an intense passion for the sensual that makes her husband, Sender (Christopher Eccleston), break into ritualistic prayers of atonement every time they get into bed together—not exactly a good harbinger for a healthy marital partnership.

When Sonia's skeevy brother-in-law Mendel (Glenn Fitzgerald) hires Sonia to be his jewelry buyer and make trips into the bustling world of Manhattan, Sonia pays a high price for even this tiny bit of freedom. Her sister-in-law (Julianna Margulies) shakes her head in disgust at Sonia's ambition, and Sender starts whining about microwaved dinners. Sonia barely gets a taste of a world where her talents and dreams are valued when she is faced with an ultimatum from her highly traditional family. Can she go it alone, or will she have to deny the most precious parts of herself in order to maintain the love and support of her family, friends, and community?

When you're feeling caged in, misunderstood, and silenced, watch *A Price Above Rubies*. You'll realize your appraisal of yourself probably needs a major upward adjustment, and watching Sonia will surely inspire your own rebellions.

It's my idea of the original sin . . . giving up.

★ Anne Bancroft as Annie Sullivan in
The Miracle Worker

■ *The Miracle Worker* (1962)
Stars: Anne Bancroft, Patty Duke, Victor Jory, Inga Swenson
Director: Arthur Penn
Writer: William Gibson, based on his play

Annie Sullivan (Anne Bancroft) really ought to insist on hardship pay from her employer: her pupil, Helen Keller (Patty Duke), slaps her, pinches her, locks her in a room, bites her, stabs her with a needle, spits on her, and wrestles her with all the force and determination of a WWF champion. Listen, after that energetic match over lunch, Captain Keller (Victor Jory) had better foot Annie's chiropractor bill and buy her a truckload of Aspercreme while he's at it.

So why does Annie put up with this treatment? Well, for one thing, Helen has an excuse for her acting out: she's a very bright child who has been deaf, mute, and blind since infancy, and now that she's in her preteen years her frustration is at a boiling point. Annie, who is nearly blind herself, has a seemingly endless well of patience, not to mention shockingly accurate insight into the Keller family dynamic. At first it appears she's just one of those spunky Irish gals who is congenitally plainspoken and self-confident, brooking no opposition. But in flashback sequences we learn that the pain of growing up in a hellish institution woefully in need of a Geraldo investigation has implanted in Annie a fierce determination to right wrongs, particularly where handicapped children are concerned. Remembering her past gives Annie the strength to handle Helen's crockery-shattering tantrums. If it takes losing a tooth and a couple of rounds before she wins the match, Annie's gonna do it. And when she does—and Helen utters and finger-spells the word *water* for the first time—you'd better have the Kleenex box at your side.

When your own battles are overwhelming, watch this movie about two strong women who triumphed despite incredible odds. May it inspire you to draw upon your anger at the injustice in your own past when you need a second wind.

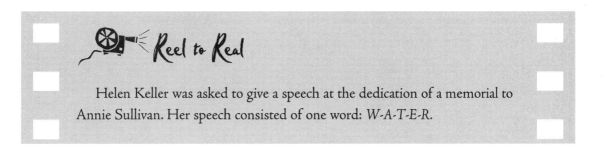

Reel to Real

Helen Keller was asked to give a speech at the dedication of a memorial to Annie Sullivan. Her speech consisted of one word: *W-A-T-E-R.*

Obedience without understanding is a blindness too.

★   Anne Bancroft as Annie Sullivan in *The Miracle Worker*

Index